PROCESS THEOLOGY AS POLITICAL THEOLOGY

Process Theology
as Political Theology

BY

JOHN B. COBB, JR.

MANCHESTER UNIVERSITY PRESS

THE WESTMINSTER PRESS

First edition

Published by
Manchester University Press
Manchester, England
and
The Westminster Press®
Philadelphia, Pennsylvania

PRINTED IN THE UNITED STATES OF AMERICA
9 8 7 6 5 4 3 2 1

This book is based on the Ferguson Lectures
delivered in the University of Manchester 1980
by Professor John B. Cobb, Jr.

Library of Congress Cataloging in Publication Data

Cobb, John B.
    Process theology as political theology.

    "Based on the Ferguson lectures delivered in the
University of Manchester 1980" — T.p. verso.
    Includes bibliographical references.
    1. Process theology.   2. Christianity and politics.
I. Title.
BT83.6.C625 1982   261.8   82-1845

ISBN (U.S.A.) 0-664-24417-3
ISBN (U.K.) 0-7190-0869-7   AACR2

CONTENTS

PREFACE

This book is about process theology and its relevance to the world of public affairs. It is written as a response to an important and impressive movement of theology into the public arena since the mid-sixties. This development has expressed itself in the theology of hope, the theology of liberation, and political theology. Each of these theologies deals with all three themes, but the choice of label usually correlates with the actual emphasis and focus.

Viewed in the light of these terms, developed chiefly in Germany and Latin America, with special contributions by Blacks and women in the United States, twentieth-century white male theology in the United States is not found entirely wanting. All three themes have been present in important ways. This has been true of the specific tradition of process theology as well. Yet in the late sixties and throughout the seventies, while continuing to contribute to discussions of hope and freedom, process theologians lagged far behind in the discussion of Christian responsibility for public affairs, especially as these are politically conceived. In relation to these topics most of our work remained abstract.[1] The theology of hope, the theology of liberation, and political theology jointly constitute a challenge to which process theology has not yet adequately responded. The distinctive thrust of this challenge appears most clearly in *political* theology. This is one reason that political theology is taken as the conversation partner in this book.

A second reason for engaging political theology instead of liberation theology can also be briefly explained. Liberation theology in its actual form and practice attends to a concrete liberation. It may be liberation of Blacks from oppression by racist society in the United States or liberation of Latin American peasants and workers from the bondage of economic colonialism and class oppression. When white representatives of the politically and economically dominant nations find themselves drawn to join forces with Blacks or Latin Americans, we are usually told that our task is to deal with our own situation, sensitive to what it is doing to others. German political theology developed in the context of the globally dominant white society, and it is accordingly more directly transferable to the situation of whites in the United States, among whom process theology so far has its primary home.[2]

A third reason for selecting political theology rather than liberation theology for discussion in this book is that other process theologians have begun the dialogue with liberation theology, and I am confident that this will continue. Two books have recently been published which considerably advance this conversation and the movement toward appropriation by process theology of central themes of liberation theology.

Schubert Ogden has published *Faith and Freedom*, which he subtitles 'Toward a theology of liberation'.[3] He describes the challenge of liberation theologies as the call 'to join them in working toward a still more adequate understanding of faith and freedom'.[4] To do so, he argues, we must distinguish without separating a double meaning in the idea of liberation. Liberation includes both redemption and emancipation.[5] Ogden identifies God's redemption as the boundless acceptance of all things, even sinners, into the divine life. Knowledge of our acceptance frees us to share in the work of emancipating people from the many bondages under which they labour. Ogden charges that most liberation theologies fail to keep this distinction clearly in mind. They tend also to focus on the meaning of God *for us*, without clarifying who and what God is as such. Each theology tends to treat only one form of bondage neglecting those treated by other liberation theologies and also narrowing the concern for liberation to human beings.

Ogden makes a clear distinction between witness and theology. Theology is critical reflection about the witness. As he sees it most of the liberation theologies are chiefly a matter of witness. This in no way depreciates their value,[6] but it does mean that another task still remains largely to be done, that is, the critical reflection about the witness which is theology as such.

The second recent book to advance the response of process theology to liberation theology significantly is Delwin Brown's *To Set at Liberty*.[7] This is not so much a critical response to the challenge of the liberation theologies as a reflection on freedom stimulated by this literature. Brown surveys the history of Western thinking about freedom and develops a contemporary formulation. He then gives expression to a theological vision centering around freedom. He formulates a doctrine of God as 'the lure toward freedom', a doctrine of sin as 'the denial of freedom', a Christology as 'the confirmation of freedom', and a soteriology as 'the future of freedom'. Throughout, he interacts appreciatively with the theologians of hope and liberation, especially Jürgen Moltmann and the Latin American liberation theologians. Although Brown does not uncritically agree with everything said by theologians of liberation, he presents his form of process theology more as a supplementation and conceptual grounding of their insights than as expressing a different understanding of the theological task.

Brown does not treat the theologians of hope and liberation as a breed apart but rather as a part of the mainstream of Christian theology in full continuity with the tradition. Similarly he does not present his own views as in contrast with theirs but rather as a contribution to working out and further developing the persuasive ideas he adopts from them. Whitehead's philosophy, he shows, far from offering an antithetical direction for theology, can deepen and ground the central commitment to liberation.

The responses of Ogden and Brown to liberation theologies quite properly centre in fresh reflections about the perennial problem of freedom. That topic is one on which process theology has always had much to say. The weakness of recent process theology is that the discussion of freedom remains somewhat abstract in relation to actual practice in political life. In order to engage political issues more directly it seems well to supplement the discussion of freedom stimulated by liberation theology with a discussion of the relation to the political sphere stimulated by political theology. In doing so I find myself working alongside David Tracy, whose *Blessed Rage for Order*[8] advocates a revisionist theology of a process mode and points forward, in a concluding chapter, to 'The *Praxis* of a revisionist theory'.

This rather lengthy explanation of the choice of political theology as dialogue partner has juxtaposed it only to liberation theology, whereas theology of hope was listed as a third form of the same general movement. The choice of political theology rather than theology of hope can be explained much more briefly. The topic of hope has been a consistent theme of process theology.[9] The weakness of process theology has been not neglect of the topic but neglect of its practical meaning for public problems. This neglect is overcome by Moltmann, whose thought thereby offers a sharp challenge to process theology. But precisely this aspect of Moltmann's work is also political theology and is recognised and named as such by him.

Whereas process theology has just begun to respond to Black and Latin American liberation theologies, the relation to the theology of women's liberation is quite different. Among the theologies that were established before the rise of the current women's movement, process theology has proved the most congenial to it. The criticisms of the classical doctrine of God by process theologians, for example, are parallel to those directed against the doctrine by women. Also the oppositions to a dualistic separation of mind and body or 'man' and nature are comparable in the two movements.[10] Process theology and feminist theology today overlap in a healthy way, and there is every indication that feminists will play leading roles in the further development of process theology.

This eminently desirable relation of process theology to this form of liberation theology, however, has not yet gone far to overcome the abstractness of process theology in relation to the political sphere. Feminists include this sphere in their concerns, and this provides further motivation for process theology to engage political theology. In dealing with political theology from the perspective of process theology it will be important to keep centrally in view what has already been learned through a partial assimilation of feminist insights.

My own journey to political theology has been through the impact of concern for the global environment. Since childhood I have been interested in politics and especially in international affairs. Later, Reinhold Niebuhr constituted my first taste of serious Christian theology, and he has been a hero for me ever since. Yet until 1969 my theology developed rather independently of my political concerns. Only my realisation in that year that the whole human race was on a collision course with disaster shook me out of this dualism and forced me to rethink my theology in light of this most inclusive question of human destiny. I found rich resources for this rethinking in the process tradition out of which I already worked, and especially in the philosophies of Alfred North Whitehead and Charles Hartshorne.

Although the questions which I was driven to raise were political in the broad sense, they came only gradually to focus on politics in the narrower sense which seemed to dominate those who called themselves political theologians. As time passed I realised that their understanding of politics was broader than I had supposed, and I increasingly saw the importance of what they were saying. But my progress was slow. The introduction to process theology which David Griffin and I wrote together in 1975 as a summary of where we had come accurately reflects the interests and concerns that had dominated our reflection prior to that time.[11] Political interests, in the narrower sense of political, were consciously omitted because we had not engaged them sufficiently to have anything distinctive to say. About that time I began working on a book with the Australian biologist Charles Birch.[12] Our shared concern was to address some of the public issues of our day from the perspective of a different understanding of the nature of reality and especially of life. The manuscript, recently completed, concludes with wide-ranging proposals for implementing the World Council of Churches call for a just, participatory and sustainable society. My work on the present book overlaps with the writing of that one, and some of the content of Chapters Five and Six is similar to short segments of the other book. It is from the perspective of these commitments, which have become increasingly controlling of my work, that I am finally ready to approach the challenge of political theology with real readiness to learn. In my case it is taking a long time to become a political theologian, and I feel a deep respect for those who found their way to this destination ahead of me. Of course the path I have followed and the journey I am still on shape the questions that I ask and lead to dissatisfaction with some of the answers that I find. My aim is to become a political theologian in the tradition of process theology.

The theologian who initiated contemporary political theology and who has most consistently attended to its development is Johann Baptist Metz. The recent writings of Metz will play the largest role in defining the position of political theology in this book. However, the term political theology has been used by others who have come to their understanding in different ways. Jürgen Moltmann and Dorothee Sölle are two of these, and some attention will be given to their writings specifically on the subject of political theology.

The book is emphatically not a critical and comprehensive study of this important movement in recent German theology or of any of its leaders. Others have provided such studies,[13] and I am dependent on their work. In the first chapter I locate this movement in relation to earlier forms of political theology and indicate its general form and emphases. I hope that enough is said for the claim that process theology, too, ought to become a political theology to be understood.

Chapter Two surveys the longer tradition at Chicago which in the past generation has been called process theology. The survey is guided by implicit attention to the challenge of political theology. The argument is that the Chicago school arose in the context of the social gospel, a movement that had much in common with contemporary political theology and that, under the stimulus of political theology, this school can recover something of what it had lost as well as move forward in new ways.

The third chapter begins the constructive task. This is the task of assimilating the rich insights already offered by political theology and relating them to the distinctive resources of process theology. This involves implicit and sometimes explicit criticism of existing formulations of political theology for what appear, from the perspective of process theology, to be lacunae or one-sided statements. The primary intention, however, is not so much to criticise this theology as to contribute to its further development. That means that the proposals inspired by the tradition of process theology are put forward in hopes of being found useful by those who have come to political theology in other ways. But whether useful to others or not, the proposals have their importance for process theology itself if it is to become a political theology. In the third chapter this constructive work centres on questions of theological method.

The fourth chapter carries on this constructive work but turns from questions of method to those of content. Process theologians are accustomed to seek conceptual clarity as grounds for existential significance. To us some of the doctrinal formulations of political theologians, while moving, do not answer questions which we cannot avoid asking. To us it seems that lack of clear answers to these questions cannot but adversely affect the movement of political theology itself in the long run. It also seems that the answers to these questions formulated by process thinkers are highly congenial to what the German political theologians are saying. In this chapter I offer process doctrines of God and eschatology in their supportive relationship to the important ideas that process theology can and should assimilate from political theologians.

Political theology has already done fine work in clarifying the relation of faith to the political sphere and in showing what the church must do in order that the appropriate relation be realised. But for a variety of reasons German theologians have been reluctant to enter the arena of political theory itself. Some of these reasons are valid, but from the point of view of a process theologian it is appropriate to go somewhat further in the direction of clarifying the principles that should guide Christians in their political aims. Chapter Five offers an expansion of principles already found in the writings of political theologians. This expansion draws on the resources of process thought.

Chapter Six discusses the scope of the political. From the perspective of process theology German political theology has dealt with reality in socio-historical terms, similar to those that dominated the first phase of the Chicago school. This is commendable. But in the past thirty or forty years, and especially during the seventies, process theology has widened its horizons so as to set human social history in the context of the entire history of life on this planet. The society of which we are a part includes the non-human world. Once this point of view has been assimilated, one cannot be satisfied with the anthropocentric perspective that underlies most of German political theology. This chapter proposes that the horizons of political theology should be so broadened that it can be formulated as an ecological theology rather than as a sociological theology.

Metz contrasts the proper work of a political theology, as a practical fundamental theology, with what he calls an evolutionary approach. What he rejects seems to include all forms of explanatory overviews of history. In Chapter Seven his position is presented and critically appraised. An alternative view of the value of a theology of history for Christian faith is offered.

An earlier version of much of the material in this book was presented in the Ferguson Lectures at the University of Manchester in
March 1980. I would like to take this opportunity to thank my hosts
there and especially Prof. and Mrs David Pailin. Some of the material,
in revised form, was also presented as the Nuveen Lectures at the
University of Chicago Divinity School and again in the Distinguished
Visiting Lectureship Program of the Department of Religious Studies
at the University of Oregon. A portion of the material was given as a
single lecture at several continental universities, and a French translation of this lecture may be published in the *Revue d'Histoire et de
Philosophie Religieuses*. A slightly different English language version
has been published in a Belgian journal.[14] There is some overlap also
with a lecture delivered at the Institute for Philosophy and Religion
at Boston University and to be published by it.

The Ferguson lectures came at an earlier point in my research on
the topics treated than I had intended. As a result I have been more
than usually dependent on the critical assistance of persons who
know the literature better than I. The assistance of Matthew Lamb
was particularly important in guiding me away from serious distortions in my representation of Metz. Bernard Meland assisted me in
coming to more accurate formulations of the development of the
Chicago school. Others who have read the entire manuscript at some
stage of its writing and given helpful responses are David Griffin,
Franklin I. Gamwell, David Vergin and Ignacio Castuera. I am grateful for assistance to typists at both the School of Theology at
Claremont and the University of Chicago Divinity School. My
assistant Jan Ritzau gave a great deal of time to bringing my foot-
notes into some semblance of order.

NOTES

1 Although this criticism must be accepted by process theologians,
process theology has never been as lacking in relevance to public
affairs as some critics have supposed. For books published in the
sixties see Note 22 to Chapter Two. During the seventies process
theologians have dealt more with environmental problems than social
ones. See books and articles by Ian Barbour, Charles Birch, John
Cobb, David Griffin, Charles Hartshorne, Schubert Ogden and others.
But during this period Widick Schroeder has continued to give leadership in the discussion of social issues. See W. Widick Schroeder,
Cognitive Structures and Religious Research: Essays in Sociology and

Theology (East Lansing, Mich.: Michigan State University, 1970). See also the collection of essays by process theologians in John B. Cobb, Jr. and W. Widick Schroeder, ed., *Process Philosophy and Social Thought* (Chicago: Center for the Scientific Study of Religion, 1981). More specific responses to the challenge of liberation theology are discussed below.

2   Moltmann, whom we will treat as a major example of 'political theology', understands his own response to the challenge of liberation theologies as also a liberation theology, this time for the oppressors. See Jürgen Moltmann with M. Douglas Meeks, 'The liberaction of oppressors', *Christianity and Crisis* (25 Dec. 1978), pp. 310–17. Sölle, another central figure in developing political theology, now describes political theology as hardly more than a step toward liberation theology. 'The development of a political theology over against a personal existentialist one was a transition; we made a first cautious step, and we still used an almost neutralized language that included ambiguities.' Dorothee Sölle, 'Resistance: toward a first World theology', *Christianity and Crisis* (23 July 1979), p. 178.

3   Schubert Ogden, *Faith and Freedom: Toward a Theology of Liberation* (Nashville, Tenn: Abingdon Press, 1979).

4   *Ibid.*, p. 43.

5   This distinction has, of course, been widely recognised. It is interesting to compare Ogden's treatment with that of Metz in 'Redemption and emancipation', first published in English in *Cross Currents* and included, in an adapted version, as Chapter 7 in *Faith in History and Society: Toward a Practical Fundamental Theology*, trans. David Smith (New York: Seabury Press, 1980).

6   Despite Ogden's intention, his formulations can appear to depreciate liberation theology. See James H. Cone, 'A critical response to Schubert Ogden's *Faith and Freedom: Toward a Theology of Liberation*', *Perkins Journal* (fall 1979), pp. 51–5.

7   Delwin Brown, *To Set at Liberty* (Maryknoll, N.Y.: Orbis Books, 1980).

8   David Tracy, *Blessed Rage for Order: the New Pluralism in Theology* (New York: Seabury Press, 1975).

9   See, e.g., Daniel Day Williams, *God's Grace and Man's Hope* (New York: Harper & Row, 1949).

10 See Sheila Davaney, ed., *Feminism and Process Thought* (New York & Toronto: Edwin Mellen Press, 1981).

11 John B. Cobb, Jr. and David R. Griffin, *Process Theology: an Introductory Exposition* (Philadelphia, Pa: Westminster Press, 1977).

12 L. Charles Birch and John B. Cobb, Jr., *The Liberation of Life* (Cambridge: University Press, 1981).

13 On Moltmann see M. Douglas Meeks, *Origins of the Theology of Hope* (Philadelphia, Pa: Fortress Press, 1974). On Metz see Roger Dick Johns, *Man in the World: the Political Theology of Johannes Baptist*

Metz (Missoula, Mont.: Scholars Press, 1976). I have not found a comparable study of Sölle. For a critical study locating contemporary political theology in the German theological context see Siegfried Wiedenhaber, *Politische Theologie* (Stuttgart: Verlag W. Kohlhammer, 1976). This includes a detailed bibliography.

14 John B. Cobb, Jr., 'Process theology and the doctrine of God', *Bijdgragen*, vol. 41, No. 4 (1980), pp. 350–67.

Chapter One

THE CHALLENGE
OF POLITICAL THEOLOGY

The main purpose of this book is to develop process theology in a way that responds appropriately to the challenge of political theology. When this is done, I claim, process theology must become a political theology. There is no intention to provide a history of political theology or to introduce the reader to the whole field of recent developments within that movement. Nevertheless, the argument cannot be understood apart from some clarification of how I perceive political theology and its challenge to process theology.

Accordingly, this chapter begins with a brief survey of the history of the term, political theology. Metz, Moltmann and Sölle are introduced in this survey, and in the second section they are presented as three more or less independent embodiments of political theology. In the third section the effort is made to distil a few common features of political theology which can determine the use of the term in the remainder of the book. These clarify also the sense in which process theology is, or should become, a political theology. The chapter concludes with brief comments on the perspective and promise of process theology in its relation to political theology.

I

The term *political theology* can be traced back to the Stoics. By them it was contrasted with mythical and natural or philosophical theology. Political theology was the expression of those religious practices which served the needs of the state. By those who held the corporate life of the people to be of supreme importance, especially in Rome, political theology was often given pride of place.

St Augustine criticised this political theology by demonstrating that there are ends beyond the state which it cannot serve. It is the City of God and not the earthly city which constitutes the true end of human beings. The affirmation of this transcendent end undercut the persuasiveness of political theology for the medieval period.

The question of society's need for religion came to the fore again during the Renaissance and the Enlightenment. Christianity's claim to a transcendent goal was seen by many as responsible for the destructive strife of the seventeenth century. The desirable religion would be one which served the needs of human community, in short, a political religion, or what Rousseau called civil religion.

The leaders of the Catholic Restoration stressed the importance of religion for society in their argument against the secularising tendencies of the Enlightenment and the French Revolution. Although at first this argument was used to support a conservative form of Catholicism, as time passed it could also be used to derive norms by which religious beliefs could be judged. Only those which have a positive social function would then be acceptable.[1]

In the twentieth century, discussion of 'political theology' was revived by Carl Schmitt who used the term as the title of a book in 1922.[2] In the chapter which also bears this title Schmitt argues for the correspondence in each epoch of the form of social authority and the theological world view. For example, he sees monarchy as correlative with theism and, indeed, the justification of monarchy as derived from theistic ideas. The supersession of monarchy by democracy is correlative with a more immanent conception of God.

Schmitt's thesis generated considerable debate. Theologians were disturbed by the suggestion that Christian teaching about God must bear responsibility for the particular forms taken by social and political authority. The major respondent to Schmitt was Erik Peterson, whose publications of 1931 and 1935[3] provided a basis for the rejection of 'political theology' by Barthains. Peterson presented Eusebius of Casesarea as the prototype of political theology and argued that the connection between theology and political doctrines of sovereignty is broken by the radical transcendence of God in Gregory of Nazianzus's doctrine of the Trinity and by Augustine's doctrine of freedom. Peterson concluded his 1935 essay with a footnote which referred to Schmitt's work and then stated: 'We have here made the attempt, to prove by a concrete example the impossibility of a "political theology" '.[4]

Nevertheless, the topic of political theology arose again in the sixties, as emphasis on the central importance of the political arena once again became influential in theological circles. In 1970 Schmitt summarised the discussion generated by his earlier book and responded in detail to Peterson's rejection of political theology.[5] In the early seventies a team of scholars sympathetic to Peterson studied the validity and the limits of his rejection of political theology and came to the conclusion that it was too conditioned by the struggle against Hitler to constitute a universal doctrine.[6]

Meanwhile another group of writings has appeared since the late sixties in which the term 'political theology' plays an important role but the debate between Schmitt and Peterson does not set the terms of the discussion. The label is used to refer to a quite different way in which theology can be related to political life. Whereas the earlier political theology sanctioned the *status quo*, the new political theology called for criticism and could support revolution.[7] It is this new type of political theology which has moved out of the German language discussion and become globally important, especially in its connection with various liberation theologies.

Johann Baptist Metz has been the key figure in the new political theology. He first used the term in his lectures in the winter terms 1965–6.[8] In his development since then and his leadership of the movement, Metz has been supported and encouraged by Jürgen Moltmann, whose 'theology of hope' struck many of the same chords.[9] Indeed, Moltmann was quite ready himself to call for a political theology. Even more than Moltmann, Dorothee Sölle has taken up the term 'political theology', presenting this as the appropriate direction for development of the Bultmannian school.[10] Sölle's influence in Germany has been chiefly in the church and among young people loosely related to the church rather than in German academic theology. Nevertheless, she has helped to shape the understanding of political theology in the English-speaking world.

Despite the difference between this form of political theology and that which had been discussed earlier, Hans Maier suggested that there are analogous weaknesses. In Maier's view Peterson's objections to political theology apply to the new form as well.

The fact that in this case the political positions supported were revolutionary rather than conservative did not remove the negative consequences of the church's effort to interfere with political life.[11]

Jürgen Moltmann, on the other hand, emphasised the difference between the new and the old meanings of political theology depicting what had earlier been called political theology as the ideology of political religion, which is the symbolic integration of the beliefs of a people through which they sanction and sanctify their traditions and their ambitions.[12] Moltmann strongly supports Peterson in his critique of political theology in this sense.[13] It is the task of what is properly called political theology — in Metz's sense — to unmask the pretenses of political religions.

Metz, too, emphasises the difference between his project and the earlier ones also called political theology and acknowledges the negative weight of using the same term. He considers the suggestion that he should speak instead of *Sozial Theologie*, *Theologie publique*, or simply *Kritische Theologie*, but he finds these alternatives still less satisfactory. The task is to give a new meaning to 'political theology' based on the changes in 'the category of the political itself in consequence of the Enlightenment'.[14] The change is to a partial separation of society from the state which leads to anti-totalitarian consequences.[15]

II

The three leading figures in German political theology with some of whose writings this book will deal are Metz, Moltmann and Sölle. They came to political theology from surprisingly different backgrounds, and these differences have some effect upon their methodologies and doctrines as these are referred to in later chapters. Since Metz is the major conversation partner in this book, more attention to him is in order, but the contrasting journeys of Moltmann and Sölle will be noted.

As a Roman Catholic theologian Metz was schooled in the tradition of transcendental Thomism.[16] This school represents the acceptance on the part of Thomists of the basic shift to the subject of knowledge entailed in the philosophy of Kant. It emphasises with Kant that the world that we know through sense experience and thought is a world that we ourselves construct. Unlike Kant, however, the transcendental Thomists have been preoccupied with the question of being. Here there is an affinity with Heidegger whose philosophy is primarily an inquiry into being on the basis of the analysis of the one who asks the question of being, that is, the human being.

The most important of the transcendental Thomists has been Karl Rahner, and Metz has been very closely associated with Rahner. Indeed, Rahner entrusted to Metz extensive revision in his earlier writings, revisions which show Metz's distinctive interest and approach. Under Rahner's tutelage Metz wrote his *Habilitationsschrift*, a study of St Thomas from the transcendental perspective, *Christliche Anthropozentrik*.[17]

In this book Metz argues that the epoch-making shift to anthropocentricity was made already in Thomas himself. The implications of this claim are enormous for the Christian understanding of modern thought. Metz views 'the modern age as the categorical carrying through of the Thomistic—Christian form of thought'.[18] Accordingly, secularisation is to be affirmed from the Christian perspective.

The extent to which Thomas did indeed inaugurate this shift so as to be the source for modern philosophy is debatable. Metz has been accused of reading back into Thomas what he learned from Kant. But this historical point need not detain us. What is important for us is Metz's own development, and his understanding of anthropocentricity is an important step in his development of a political theology.

He distinguishes between the content of a philosophy and its controlling understanding of being. Much Greek thought, for example, focuses on the human being and is, in this sense, anthropocentric in its content. But it views human beings in an objectifying way because its controlling understanding of being is taken from the objects of experience. For this reason Metz calls it cosmocentric.

In contrast to this he finds that the content of Thomas's thought is God, and it may accordingly be described as theocentric. But Thomas has turned away from the object of experience to subjectivity itself for his fundamental grasp of what being is. This constitutes St Thomas as anthropocentric in the sense with which Metz is fundamentally concerned.[19]

The world does not exist in itself over against human beings. It has its being in and as the self-externalisation of human beings. Similarly God is not an object existing above human beings but is the transcendental subjectivity of human subjectivity. '"To come before God" is at once the highest form of man's "coming to himself", the fulfilment of his subjectivity.'[20]

In the mid-sixties Metz concentrated on the understanding of the world. Although the world does not exist apart from human beings, this does not make it a private matter. 'Every experience of the world takes place within the horizon of shared human existence, not merely in the "private" sense of the I-thou, but in the "political" sense of social existence in community. Thus every experience of the world and the interpretation of the world based on it are inter-subjectively or intercommunicatively grounded.'[21] The context for understanding the world is human history.

The theology of the world thus moves directly into political theology. 'The theology of the world is neither a purely objectivistic theology of the cosmos nor a purely transcendental theology of the person and existence. It is a political theology. The creative — militant hope behind it is related essentially to the world as society and to the forces within it that change the world.'[22]

Meanwhile Metz's way of thinking of God was also changing. In *Christliche Anthropozentrik* God as the final end of human beings was thought of as the ground and content of future human fulfilment. Hence the note of futurity was present, but it was not central. But when Metz addressed the question of God again toward the end of the sixties he did so entirely in the context of the Christian hope for the coming of God. God is indissolubly related to the realm of freedom and peace that is promised and that comes to believers now as the call to realise freedom and peace concretely in our world.[23]

A collection of essays written from 1961 to 1967 was published under the title *Theology of the World*.[24] These include an article entitled 'The church and the world in the light of a "Political theology"'. It was this essay that launched the extended discussion of Metz's new 'political theology'.

Already by 1969 this discussion gave rise to a book which also gave Metz the opportunity to reply to his critics.[25] In this reply he provides a clearer statement of what he takes as the cardinal features of a political theology than he had included in the initial essay. He identifies three. The first is the task of a 'theological hermeneutic in the contemporary social context'.[26] This can be called a political hermeneutic. Second, the new political theology should be a 'critical corrective over against a certain privatizing tendency in recent theology'.[27] And third, since theology and the church actually have massive political importance, political theology must have a 'critical function in the church'.[28]

Jürgen Moltmann followed a quite different, and in many ways more direct, road to political theology. Deeply stamped by his experience as a prisoner of war, he returned to Germany after World War II to study theology. Referring to himself in the third person he writes briefly of how he was shaped during that period:

> This student sat at the feet of Gerhard von Rad, Ernst Käsemann, Hans Joachim Iwand, Ernst Wolf, and Otto Weber at the University of Göttingen. There he imbibed the theology of the Confessing Church, inspired by Karl Barth and preserved throughout the years of struggle between the church and the Nazi state ... We learned the origin of the Christian faith in the suffering of him who was crucified and in the liberating power of the risen Christ ... We could withstand the crucifying experiences of life only through faith in the vicarious suffering and death of Christ our brother, and in the freedom conferred by his resurrection. That is what made us so Christocentric. Barth's theology was simply the first and most enlightening formulation of faith in such experiences. That is why we didn't become Barthians, but with gratitude went beyond him toward the eschatological, toward the theology of the cross, and toward a politically critical theology.[29]

It was with this eschatological emphasis within a Barthian matrix of thought that Moltmann encountered the work of Ernst Bloch. He found in Bloch a philosophical conceptuality that enabled him to draw loose ends together and to understand his own intentions. Hence Bloch, and through Bloch the humanistic Marxist tradition, became the second great source of Moltmann's thought.

From such sources it is not difficult to see how there emerged a 'theology of hope'. The tendency of Barth's eschatology to relativise the importance of history by picturing God as above, instead of in the future, had to be overcome. Bloch's 'atheism' also had to be dealt with. But much of the needed work was already accomplished by his Göttingen teachers. It remained for Moltmann to bring the whole together in a new form with the stamp of his own experience and thought upon it.

The term *political* was not prominent in *The Theology of Hope*, but the substance was already there. Hence no real change was involved when in the years after its publication Moltmann began to speak of his as a political theology, associating himself closely with the position of Metz.

In 1971 Moltmann published an essay on 'Political theology' in which he undertook to explain it to the English-speaking world. He points out that Christians now have considerable freedom in relation to our own traditions but that we have not attained similar freedom in relation to the political world.

> Consequently modern criticism asks about the practical, political, and psychic effects of the churches, of theologies, and of ways of believing. Responsible theology must therefore engage in institutional criticism as it reflects on the 'place' of the churches 'in the life' of modern society and in ideological criticism as it reflects on itself. It can no longer self-forgetfully screen out its own social and political reality as the old metaphysical and personalistic theologies did ... Political theology designates the field, the milieu, the environment, and the medium in which Christian theology should be articulated today.[30]

Alongside and expressive of this understanding of political theology as politically self-critical theology is the view of political theology as hermeneutical. Form criticism has already made us aware of the social setting of our texts. As we become equally conscious of the social setting in which we stand, we can develop a political hermeneutic. 'We can move from the existentialist and personalistic interpretations of traditional texts to a political hermeneutic of these traditions and from a hermeneutic of pure understanding to an exegesis of traditional religious representations in practical intent.'[31]

Dorothee Sölle came to political theology from existentialist theology. She studied theology, along with German philology, at Göttingen and Freiburg. Her most influential teachers were Friedrich Gogarten and Ernst Käsemann. In 1965, the same year in which Moltmann published *The Theology of Hope*, she published her first book, *Christ the Representative: an Essay in Theology after the 'Death of God'*.[32] She was impressed, like Metz, with the secularisation of modern experience and recognised that this entailed a sense of the absence or "death" of God. She wanted to show how modern people can still find their identity in Christ as their representative.

Two years later Sölle published *Phantasie und Gehorsam*, translated into English as *Beyond Mere Obedience*.[33] Her movement towards political theology is manifest in this book as she shows how the close association of faith with blind obedience to God, encouraged by much Christian theology, correlates with the obedience to human rulers manifest in Germany in the Nazi period. She calls instead for the strengthening of personal selfhood and the prizing of self-realisation and personal fulfilment which express themselves in creative spontaneity and fantasy. In one chapter, placed as an appendix in the English translation, Sölle directly anticipates her future work by arguing that demythologising or existential interpretation does not suffice. 'A demythology which does not become an ideological critique reinforces the ideological veil that hangs above our social reality simply because its partial explanations create an elite sense of complete enlightenment.'[34]

Sölle cannot share with Metz and Moltmann the apocalyptic language which implies that God will eventually bring a universal fulfilment. But this does not lessen for her the importance of what is happening now to human beings in our world. For some years, before dealing directly with the topic of political theology, Sölle was leader of 'Politisches Nachtgebet' in Cologne. This was a group which met once a month for political worship, that is, for analysis of particular social crises and reflection and prayer about them, followed by asking what could be done in response.

In 1970 Sölle addressed the meeting of Old Marburgers on the relation of Bultmann's hermeneutical method to political theology. Her book *Political Theology* grew out of that lecture and subsequent discussions. In it political theology is pictured as the consistent outcome and development of Bultmann's critical method derived from the Enlightenment. In the Enlightenment this method was employed politically. Whereas some of Bultmann's followers have developed a kerygmatic orthodoxy based on identifying the kerygma with a body of fixed doctrines, Bultmann's intention was to contrast the kerygma to doctrine and to keep all doctrine subject to criticism. This intention is better fulfilled when the full breadth of Enlightenment criticism is recovered. This would involve moving from the existing recognition of the socio-political character of the text in its original setting to that of the socio-political meaning of the text in the contemporary setting as well.

Sölle does not provide us with a convenient list of the essential features of political theology. Where she deals most explicitly with this question she focuses on hermeneutic. She states that political theology is best understood as 'political interpretation of the gospel'.[35] But there are other ingredients clearly indicated.

For Sölle, as for Metz and Moltmann, political theology is essentially critical theology. It is critical of theology and of the church. It is also critical of existing structures of society. Finally, it involves self-criticism, the acknowledgement of how one is bound up in the sin of society and has the tendencies which lead to the most vicious acts. 'A criticism of society which ... does not detect and give expression to the capitalist or to the concentration camp guard that is in each of us, but instead creates enemies in hostile projections, I consider political propaganda, plain and simple, and not a political interpretation of the gospel.'[36]

Sölle is as clear as Metz and Moltmann that political theology is not the substitution of political ideas for theology. But she does note that there is a place for a constructive role in relation to the political world. She describes this as 'projecting innovative models'.[37]

III

There are important theological differences among these three leaders of political theology, and it will be necessary to discuss some of them. But what is striking is that, despite their diverse journeys to political theology, their views of what this is are so similar. All three see political theology as a hermeneutic. All three see it as criticism of church and theology. And although deprivatisation is not an express theme of Moltmann and Sölle, it is implicit in their whole programmes.

On one very important point with respect to the understanding of political theology, however, differences do appear. None of them see political theology as merely the expression in the political arena of a theology that in its core is not political. But the question remains whether all theology is or should be political theology, whether the political is the sole horizon for theological work. The critical question is whether personal salvation can be fully subsumed under political salvation.

Sölle is quite clear that today all theology should be political theology. She writes: 'The theological program that must be undertaken is called "political theology" — specifically one that understands itself not as a mere component but as the essential formulation of the theological problem for our time.'[38] This follows consistently from her view that there is no individual salvation.

> Political theology begins with a modified preunderstanding. Its guiding hermeneutical principle is the question of authentic life for all men. This does not mean that the question about individual existence must be suppressed or thrust aside as nonessential. But surely even that question can be answered only in terms of social conditions and in the context of social hopes. No one can be saved alone. Subjectivity is injected into even this process of social understanding, but not for the purpose of seeking understanding, for itself alone; rather it believes in and calls for the indivisible salvation of the whole world.[39]

This view of the indivisibility of salvation for all is consistently rooted in the conviction that 'all reality is worldly and inherently social'.[40]

That political theology is the inclusive form of theology does not imply that there is a lack of interest in individuals. Political theology does not reject the insights attained by existential theology. Indeed, Sölle claims that 'political theology reveals for the first time the truth of existentialist theology, because it enables and does not merely postulate an existential way of speaking, which also concerns the individual'.[41] She illustrates this as follows: 'It is not enough to criticize property rights ... so long as we, as "powerless" individuals, are not able to clarify how we are entangled in the general structures, that is, how we profit from the structures and how we conform to the introverted norms that we regard as self-evident — for example, the norms of achievement, consumerism, reasons of state — and pass them on to others, even when we reject them privately and verbally.'[42] But this existential meaning of the message of political theology clearly does not require the development, alongside political theology, of another, oriented to the individual.

In Moltmann's case the situation is different. There is no lack of emphasis on the salvation of the whole world, and as in Sölle this is presented in such a way as to bring out its existential meaning. But the treatment of the individual is not exhausted by the existential meaning of the political message. For example, the two concluding chapters of *The Crucified God* deal respectively with 'Ways towards the psychological liberation of man' and 'Ways towards the political liberation of man'.[43] Although Moltmann is very sensitive to the socio-historical context of psychiatry, it does not seem that he wants to subsume the psychological entirely under the heading of the political.

If for Moltmann the political is not the one horizon for all theology, this can be explained by the fact that he does conceive of an individual liberation or salvation as well as the inclusive one. He writes that the 'inner poisoning of life extends not only through poor societies but through rich societies as well. It cannot therefore be overcome simply by victory over economic need, political oppression, cultural alienation and the ecological crisis. Nor can it be reduced to these realms and dimensions ... This would remain open in the best of all conceivable societies. It can only be healed by the presence of meaning in all events and relationships of life'. [44] Also 'the liberation of the believer from the prison of sin, law and death, is brought by God, not by politics'.[45] This presupposes a relation of the individual to the corporate quite different from that affirmed by Sölle.

Metz seems to be closer to Sölle than to Moltmann on this topic. To view political theology as one branch of theology alongside others would be, from his point of view, to miss the point. This theology is a new way of implementing the total theological task. In Metz's words, political theology 'tries to carry out the same task that Christian theology has always carried out — that of speaking about God by making the connection between the Christian message and the modern world'. It 'is not simply a theory of the subsequent application of the Christian message, but a theory of the truth of that message'. It 'does not aim to be a regional task of contemporary theology as a whole but a fundamental task'. [46]

If Metz does agree with Sölle on this important point, this is consistent with his anthropology. Metz views the human situation as inherently social. If there is no existence that is not bound up with others, then there can be no salvation apart from the salvation of others. The social or political horizon is truly fundamental for the understanding of all things human.

Nevertheless, Metz's statements on this point are not quite as unequivocal as Sölle's. He recognises a distinction between "the one history of salvation and the many histories of salvation and the absence of salvation of individuals' although he believes that they 'merge together without diminishing each other'.[47] This *could* open the way for supplementing the political horizon with a psychological one.

What such supplementation would mean is shown by the work of one of his students, Francis Fiorenza. In his discussion of political theology as a fundamental theology, Fiorenza adopts the view that there is a duality of goals. He affirms that 'political theology represents only one horizon and not the sole horizon of theology as a foundational theology'.[48] He requires, in addition, existential and transcendental horizons. These horizons can be analysed in reference to their societal and political dimension, but this in no way denies their significance as distinct horizons. The political and the existential are each more extensive than the other. Existential questions of birth, life and death transcend the societal and cannot be politically resolved. Nor can every political issue be reduced to an existential question.'[49]

This view of multiple horizons is plausible, but it is doubtful that it can be attributed to Metz. Metz went to some length in his earlier writings to do away with the transcendental horizon in so far as it could be juxtaposed to the socio-political one as Fiorenza suggests. Further, he would not be happy to set the existential alongside the political in this way. He perceives the existential interest as the heir of Enlightenment individualism. This individualism was bound up with the critical spirit which he strongly commends. But in Metz's account the individuals of Enlightenment individualism are bourgeois individuals conceived in abstraction from the social circumstances which make autonomy and maturity possible for them. Theology written by and for such individuals fails to deal with the problem of how what they are called to be could become possible for other human beings. It also idealises a form of individual self-realisation that undercuts solidarity with all humanity.[50] Metz would probably see a theology which paired existential and political horizons as yielding too much to our bourgeois complacency.

One factor entering into the complexity of this argument is the lack of clear definition of 'political'. Sometimes all human activity and thought is called political in that it is denied that any of it is free of political consequences. From this it follows that psychological or existential liberation is also political. But political theology, it seems, calls attention to that public effect. Accordingly, the only norms which could be applied to the experience of psychological liberation by the political theologian in the narrow sense would be those of its public or social effects.

Even in the public sphere there is an ambiguity in the use of the term *political*. Again it is used broadly so that even such apparently non-political activities as efforts to re-think Christianity in the light of discussions with Buddhists can be viewed as political activity. Yet the choice of the term *political* has a marked tendency to direct attention elsewhere. Those who call themselves political theologians have not been in the forefront of the interreligious dialogue. Some of them, especially Metz, have yet to show much interest in the liberation of women. The emphasis on the 'political' directs them to socio-economic and international affairs instead. The breadth of Moltmann's interests may be one reason that the term *political* does not appear as the encompassing horizon of his theology, even though he is never oblivious to the political dimension, in the narrower sense, of what he is doing.

For all political theologians theory is in the service of practice. This practice is not, of course, blind activism. It is activity informed by thought. What is important is that thought should not be viewed as an end in itself or as the means for gaining truths which are only subsequently related to action in the world. As Christians we engage in reflection, even quite abstract reflection, because we need to act and to act rightly. This action is, of course, political action.

Furthermore, for political theologians practice is guided and governed by a global perspective. They are citizens not of one country but of the whole world.[51] The church and theology are criticised in terms of how they function in the global scene. Political theologians seek the salvation of all humanity.

There is no Christian imperialism here. Salvation is not sought by incorporating everyone into the Christian church. But Christians view the acceptability of their institutions and doctrines in terms of their meaning for the whole human race.

This global perspective contrasts not only with political theologies of the past which correlated theology with the needs of particular states, but also with liberation theologies. These begin with an analysis of some concrete oppression. They mobilise energy for liberation from that oppression. They acknowledge, of course, the global horizon of their ultimate concern, but this does not relate directly to their major task which is to deal with the actuality of a particular social situation.

In this comparison much is to be said for the advantage of liberation theologies. They can have an actual social effectiveness which is largely lacking in political theologies. These latter cannot concentrate energies over a sustained period on a single issue or task. As a result they give the impression of dilettantism. What they can do is to create a climate of support for many different activities of liberation.

IV

Process theology ought to become a political theology. For a few, this political theology may take the form of a liberation theology. But most male white North American process theologians will not become liberation theologians for the same reason that the German theologians are not liberation theologians. As members of the dominant society our task is to become aware of how we, as citizens, as theologians and as churches, share in sustaining and strengthening the structures of oppression and destruction which govern our world. That requires of us the politically self-critical stance that is essential to political theology. It requires also deprivatisation of our understanding of human existence and of salvation. It requires that political understanding be brought to the interpretation of the scriptures and of the entire tradition. Furthermore, it requires that we should think for the sake of Christian living and that we should understand our Christian practice in global perspective. Process theology should become a political theology in that it should be fundamentally committed, with Sölle, to 'the indivisible salvation of the whole world'. [52]

Process theology cannot follow Sölle in viewing the political horizon as the only one, but it can learn to share with Moltmann in giving pervasive and central attention to it. The understanding of human beings as indissolubly social is at least as basic for process thought as for either Sölle or Metz. Hence, intrinsic to process theology is a deep sympathy for their emphasis. But the exclusive claims sometimes made would have to be formulated very carefully before process theology could accept them. The tendency of the term *political* to highlight particular segments of the public world can be approved, because of the importance of these segments, but emphasis must fall also on the importance of relationships between women and men, of resolving misunderstandings between Christians and Hindus, of deepening our understanding of how we are related to other animals, of providing emotional support to a friend in time of crisis.[53]

The important contributions made to practice by thought which seeks only truth would need to be stressed. We would have to clarify the real and important gains that can be made by limited communities even when the remainder of humanity is little benefited. Since process theologians believe that every individual is immediately related to God, formulations which *identify* the relationship to God with that to humanity or the hoped-for future would require revision. And since process theology sees human beings as part of a larger community which includes all creatures, the indivisible salvation of the whole world cannot be limited to humanity.

Such qualifications do not constitute a rejection of political theology. But they do show that process theology as a political theology will have distinctive character. It is with this assumption that this book is written. The next chapter examines the rise of process theology within the Chicago school in the light of the need for process theology to become a political theology.

NOTES

1 For a much more detailed and precise account of the history of 'political theology' prior to the twentieth century, see Francis Fiorenza, 'Political theology as foundational theology', The Catholic Theological Society of America, *Proceedings of the Thirty-Second Annual Convention* (Bronx, N. Y.: CTSA, 1977), pp. 147–66.
2 Carl Schmitt, *Politische Theologie: Vier Kapitel zur Lehre von der Souveränität* (Munich and Leipzig: Duncker & Humblot, 1922).
3 Erik Peterson, 'Göttliche Monarchie', *Theologischen Quartalsschrift*, Heft LV (1931), pp. 537–64; and Erik Peterson, *Der Monotheismus als politisches Problem; ein Beitrag zur Geschichte der politschen Theologie im Imperium Romanum* (Leipzig: Jakob Hegner, 1935).
4 Erik Peterson,*Theologische Traktate* (Munich' Kösel Verlag, 1950), p. 147.
5 Carl Schmitt, *Politische Theologie II: die Legende von der Erledigung jeder Politischen Theologie* (Berlin: Duncker & Humblot, 1970).

6   See, for example, Alfred Schindler, ed., *Monotheismus als politisches Problem? Erik Peterson und die Kritik der politischen Theologie* (Gütersloh: Gütersloher Verlagshaus Ger Mohn, 1978).

7   See, for example, the essays collected under the title *Politische Theologie*, Tutzinger Texte, No. 7 (Munich: Claudius Verlag, 1970).

8   Roger Dick Johns, *Man in the World: the Political Theology of Johannes Baptist Metz* (Missoula, Mont.: Scholars Press, 1976), p. 123.

9   Jürgen Moltmann, *Theology of Hope*, trans. James W. Leitch (New York: Harper & Row, 1967).

10 Dorothee Sölle, *Political Theology*, trans. John Shelley (Philadelphia, Pa: Fortress Press, 1971).

11 Hans Maier, 'Politische Theologie? Einwände eines Laien', in *Diskussion zur 'Politischen Theologie'*, ed. Helmut Peukert (Mainz: Matthias-Grünewald Verlag and Munich: Chr. Kaiser Verlag, 1969); Hans Maier, *Kritik der Politischen Theologie* (Einsiedeln: Johannes Verlag, 1970).

12 Jürgen Moltmann, 'Theologische Kritik der Politische Religion', in J.B. Metz, Jürgen Moltmann, and Willi Oelmüller, *Kirche im Prozess der Aufklärung: Aspekte einer neuen 'politsche Theologie'* (Munich: Chr. Kaiser Verlag, 1970), pp. 11–51.

13 Jürgen Moltmann, 'Political theology,' in *The Experiment Hope*, trans. M. Douglas Meeks (Philadelphia, Pa: Fortress Press, 1975), pp. 106–8.

14 Johann Baptist Metz, ' "Politische Theologie" in der Diskussion', in *Diskussion zur 'Politischen Theologie'*, ed. Helmut Peukert (Mainz: Matthias-Grünewald Verlag and Munich: Chr. Kaiser Verlag, 1969), p. 269. (My translation).

15 *Ibid.*, p. 270. A careful summary of the relation of the recent discussion to the earlier one up to 1974 is found in Frithard Scholz, 'Bemerkungen zur Funktion der Peterson — These in der neueren Diskussion um Politische Theologie', in Schindler, *op. cit.*, pp. 170–201.

16 I am indebted to Johns, *Man in the World*, for the following summary of Metz's development. He provides a far more detailed account.

17 Johann Baptist Metz, *Christliche Anthropozentrik: Über die Denkform des Thomas von Aquin* (Munich: Kösel Verlag, 1962).

18 *Ibid.*, p. 124. (My translation.)

19 *Ibid.*, p. 47.

20 *Ibid.*, p. 80. (My translation.)

21 Johann Baptist Metz, 'Welt', *Lexikon für Theologie und Kirche*, cols. 1024–5, trans. by Johns in *Man in the World*, p. 90.

22 'The Responsibility of Hope,' *Philosophy Today*, 1966, p. 287.

23 'Der Zukünftige Mensch und der Kommende Gott', in Hans Jürgen Schulz, ed. *Wer ist das eigentlich—Gott?* (Munich: Kosel-Verlag, 1969). See especially pp. 267–75.

24 Johann Baptist Metz, *Theology of the World*, trans. William Glen-Doepel (New York: Herder & Herder, 1971).

18

25 In Peukert, *Diskussion zur 'Politischen Theologie'*.
26 *Ibid.*, P. 274. (My translation.)
27 *Ibid.*, p. 275. (My translation.)
28 *Ibid.*, p. 277. (My translation.)
29 Jürgen Moltmann, 'Foreword' in M. Douglas Meeks, *Origins of the Theology of Hope* (Philadelphia, Pa.: Fortress Press, 1974), pp. xi–xii. I am indebted to Meeks for much of this account. See also Moltmann's autobiographical statement in *Experiences of God*, trans. Margaret Kohl (Philadelphia, Pa.: Fortress Press, 1980), pp. 6–17.
30 Jürgen Moltmann, *The Experiment Hope*, pp. 102–3.
31 *Ibid*:, p. 103.
32 Dorothee Sölle, *Christ the Representative: an Essay in Theology after the 'Death of God'*, trans. David Lewis (Philadelphia, Pa.: Fortress Press, 1967).
33 Dorothee Sölle, *Beyond Mere Obedience: Reflections on a Christian Ethic for the Future*, trans. Lawrence W. Denet (Minneapolis, Minn.: Augsburg Press, 1971).
34 *Ibid.*, p. 85.
35 Dorothee Sölle, *Political Theology*, p. 56.
36 *Ibid.*, p. 92.
37 *Ibid.*, p. 76.
38 *Ibid.*, p. 2.
39 *Ibid.*, p. 60.
40 *Ibid.*, p. 67.
41 *Ibid.*, p. 92.
42 *Ibid.*, p. 92.
43 Jürgen Moltmann, *The Crucified God*, trans. R.A. Wilson and John Bowden (New York: Harper & Row, 1974), chapters 7 and 8.
44 *Ibid.*, pp. 334–5.
45 *Ibid.*, pp. 319–20. Moltmann also writes on 'The theology of mystical experience', in *Experiences of God*, pp. 55–80. Although he associates Christian mysticism with a discipleship that is also political, the positive appraisal of contemplation widens the boundaries of political theology.
46 Johann Baptist Metz, *Faith in History and Society: Toward a Practical Fundamental Theology*, trans. David Smith (New York: Seabury Press, 1980), p. 89.
47 *Ibid.*, p. 165.
48 Francis Fiorenza, 'Political theology as foundational theology', pp. 146–7 (see Note 1).
49 *Ibid.*, p. 146.
50 Metz, *Faith in History and Society*, pp. 27–8.
51 *Ibid.*, p. 4.
52 Sölle, *Political Theology*, p. 60.
53 The broad use of 'political theology' here called for is taken for granted in *The Scope of Political Theology*, ed. Alastair Kee (London: SCM Press Ltd., 1978). It is assumed also in "Political theology: a documentary and bibliographical survey" published in *WCC Exchange*, October 1977.

Chapter Two

PROCESS THEOLOGY IN VIEW
OF THE CHALLENGE
OF POLITICAL THEOLOGY

Process theology has several overlapping meanings. The term came into currency in the fifties. It referred to the type of theology that had developed at Chicago especially under the influence of the philosophy of Alfred North Whitehead. But the term was readily adopted by others, for example, the followers of Teilhard de Chardin. It may be helpful to indicate three ways in which the label can be used and then to select one of them for the remainder of the chapter.

Process theology may refer to all forms of theology that emphasise event, occurrence, or becoming over against substance. In this sense theology influenced by Hegel is process theology just as much as that influenced by Whitehead. This use of the term calls attention to affinities between these otherwise quite different traditions. Much of Biblical theology, especially when it stresses the difference between Biblical modes of thought and Greek philosophical categories, has belonged to process theology in this broad sense. Most political theology also is a form of process theology thus understood.

Again *process theology* may mean theology which systematically employs the philosophical conceptuality of Alfred North Whitehead or Charles Hartshorne. Certainly theology of this sort is called process theology and has been a major contribution to the development of the movement. My own book *A Christian Natural Theology*[1] contributed to this way of understanding process theology.

Finally, *process theology* may refer to a theological movement that developed at the University of Chicago Divinity School during the thirties. This is much narrower than the first use and overlaps extensively with the second. The movement emerged as the influence of Whitehead was felt at Chicago, but many of the participants are not best understood as Whiteheadians in a narrow sense. Yet their emphasis on 'process' has not been less than his.

I shall follow this third usage, noting how Whitehead's influence grew in this tradition to the point that the third usage has almost merged with the second. Indeed, since the 'Chicago school' is no longer strong at Chicago, there is an increasing tendency for the balance to shift toward the second usage of process theology. But for the present, the continuing influence among process theologians of members of the Chicago school whose positions are related to that of Whitehead quite loosely, argues for the importance of understanding process theology in relation to its historical origins at Chicago.

The history of the Chicago school can be described in three phases. The first phase lasted from the establishment of the school until around 1930 and its unity lies in the concern for the socio-historical method. Shailer Mathews typifies the theology of this phase, and Section I will describe it with special attention to him. In many ways this phase was closer to political theology than its successors have been.

Although the idea of process, and, indeed, the term *process*, were very prominent in this first phase, *process theology* has rarely been used to describe the socio-historical school. This label refers more to the second and third phases. The second phase was initiated by the coming to Chicago in the late twenties of Henry Nelson Wieman and Charles Hartshorne. Sections II and III summarise their distinctive contributions. Both were influenced by Whitehead; so the merging of the Chicago tradition with Whiteheadian theology began then. But their own positions were quite sharply distinct, one being radically empiricist, and the other, rationalist.

A third phase of the Chicago school can be identified as that of the leadership of the students of Wieman and Hartshorne. This phase overlaps chronologically with the second, since some of their students began teaching at Chicago while Wieman and Hartshorne were still there. As a matter of convenience we may think of this phase, rather arbitrarily, as beginning around 1950. Both Wieman and Hartshorne continued their teaching careers elsewhere after leaving Chicago, and most of their students also taught elsewhere. Hence this phase is one in which 'the Chicago school' gradually ceased to be closely identified with Chicago and was increasingly identified instead by the label *process theology*. Section IV deals with this phase. It illustrates the diversity within this phase by briefly identifying three of its leaders who did teach, at least for a while, at Chicago. It also raises the question of the relation of process theology to the political concerns that had governed the first phase of the school. The intention is in part to display the distance between this process theology and political theology at the time the latter arose in Germany. It is also to indicate the distinctive perspective and resources which process theology brings to the questions raised for it by political theology.

I

A Baptist divinity school was moved to the site of the present University of Chicago to become the nucleus of the university in 1892. William Rainey Harper, a Biblical scholar, became the first president of the university and proceeded self-consciously to develop a new type of university. It was, on the one hand, to be chiefly oriented to graduate education and, on the other hand, to be related to the actual situation of the American Mid-west. The features of the situation that seemed most important to the Divinity School faculty were the social stresses caused by industrialisation and the growing sense among the public of the irrelevance of the Bible. The latter was perceived as partly due to changes in the intellectual climate, but as chiefly due to the interpretation of the Bible in an individualistic and unhistorical way, which made it irrelevant to the social problems of the times.

To describe the Divinity School faculty's perception of the problem in this way is to say little more than that it participated in the Social Gospel movement which was gaining wide influence at the time. That movement had its unity not in a theology but in the conviction that the Christian churches had the responsibility to address the injustices of the class society being produced by industrialisation and that the Bible, properly understood, required concern for these social issues. It is striking that when Walter Rauschenbusch finally gave lectures in 1917 on 'A theology for the social gospel', he began by saying: 'We have a social gospel. We need a systematic theology large enough to match it and vital enough to back it.'[2]

This subordination of theology to the church's social mission sounded out-of-date in the next generation, but it is strikingly similar to the writing of many present-day political theologians. Black theologians such as James Cone understand theology as appropriate only as it serves the cause of Black liberation. Latin American theologians find, like Rauschenbusch, that there is a movement of liberation already in motion and that their task is to develop a 'theology large enough to match it and vital enough to back it'. Dorothee Sölle begins her lectures on 'Political theology' by quoting from Bonhoeffer's prophesy addressed to us: 'For your thought and action will enter on a new relationship; your thinking will be confined to your responsibilities in action. With us thought was often the luxury of the onlooker; with you it will be entirely subordinated to action.'[3]

Political and liberation theologies are certainly not mere repetitions of the theology of the earlier Social Gospel. Many of the issues that they emphasise are different. They respond to a different theological history. Nevertheless, as process theology now encounters the challenge of political theology, its roots in the earlier period of the Chicago school take on a new currency and relevance.

It was at Chicago that the methodological implications of the social gospel were most fully worked out by what was called the socio-historical school. Christianity was viewed as an historical movement developing out of Judaism under the impact of Jesus's person and teaching. Doctrines were thought to have been formulated as needed to support the efforts of the movement in meeting perceived needs. These formulations were thus in the categories and concepts appropriate for the time and for the sake of providing sanction and guidance for the task at hand.

In the view of the socio-historical school the systematic task in the modern world is the same. Those who are immersed in the Christian movement need to formulate teachings that assist it in fulfilling its current calling. The advocates of the socio-historical method perceived that calling to be support of the oppressed classes in their struggle for justice. Hence doctrines of God and Christ and ecclesiology were to be shaped in such a way as to encourage and aid the church in this task.

When the church is seen in this way the primary question about its teachings is not their truth or accuracy. The primary test is functional or pragmatic. Does the doctrine aid in achieving the current goals of the movement? But a formulation which is not in the idiom of the day and which does not seem plausible and even convincing is of little use. Hence appropriateness to the best current thinking is an important norm. Theology must be formulated in the terms of the social mind of the time, which meant, for the Chicago thinkers, in democratic categories and thought forms shaped by the influence of modern science. In this context faith must be expressed in relevant imagery capable of evoking and informing understanding and impelling commitment.

Similarly the primary question is not that of faithfulness to Biblical formulations. The Christian movement must state the doctrines it now needs whether or not these can be derived directly from the Bible. Nevertheless, in a movement which looks back to the records of its origins for inspiration, it is important to show the connection of current teaching to the Scriptures. Hence scholarly attention at the Chicago Divinity School focused on the Bible.

This Biblical study was done under the aegis of the socio-historical method. The Bible tells and reflects the history of a movement. Its teachings reflect the needs and goals of that movement at various times in its socio-historical development. The modern study of the Bible can bring that history to life for us today and renew our zest in continuing the movement of whose origins and early history it tells us.

Perhaps the finest scholar of the school was Shirley Jackson Case. His book *The Evolution of Early Christianity: a Genetic Study of First Century Christianity in Relation to its Religious Environment*, published in 1914, was a manifesto of the socio-historical programme. Case recognised his indebtedness to Ernst Troeltsch, but he was also quite conscious of his differences. Case objected that 'Troeltsch can speak of an "essential" Christianity in whose history the fundamental "ideal" is being realized through progress toward the "absolute goal" '.[4] Case had no place for an essence, a fundamental ideal or an absolute goal. He knew nothing but the socio-historical phenomena themselves.

Although Case gave some of the clearest statements of the implications of the socio-historical method, the man who best typifies the Divinity School and most influenced its development through the first three decades of this century was Shailer Mathews. Two years after the establishment of the Divinity School he was called from his position in history and political economy at Colby College to teach New Testament history and, after 1906, theology. In 1908 he became Dean of the Divinity School, a post he held until his retirement in 1933.

Mathews approached New Testament history from a perspective developed as a student of history and politics. This perspective had been sharpened by a year's study at Berlin, but it is striking that his interests at that time were such that he did not attend any lectures in theology, even those of Harnack.[5] Although he developed great appreciation for Harnack in later years, he worked out his own approach to Biblical scholarship by applying to the scriptures methods developed with other subject matters in view. One of his first books was an interpretation of the French Revolution as a socio-historical movement — a book widely used in American high schools for a quarter of a century — and his approach to Christianity was also as a socio-historical movement, even a revolutionary one.

Mathews's lack of advanced education in Biblical scholarship of his day resulted in a certain naivete in his work. But this naivete was also its strength. Mathews could apply the socio-historical methodology to the Bible without the theological anxieties that characterised more sophisticated scholars. The struggle to reconcile faith and history was lacking. He assumed that history has the last word. But the history that has the last word is that of a living movement in which the historian participates.

Mathews saw Christianity as a social movement inspired by Jesus and striving for the realisation of such values as sacrificial love. Like all religions it is a means of adjusting life to social reality. Its doctrines are a by-product of its life, and they therefore require repeated transformation as society and knowledge change and grow. The attempt to identify a constant kernel of belief is illusory and leads to distortion in the interpretation of the past.

Mathews traced the development of Christianity in the context of successive 'social minds'.[6] Christianity arose in the context of the Semitic social mind, and developed through the Greco-Roman, the imperialist, the feudal, the nationalist, and the bourgeois social minds. It now exists in the context of the modern social mind. This mind is characterised by democracy on the one side and the scientific method on the other. The task of formulating the faith in this emerging context is now before the Christian movement.

Mathews saw himself as a part of this movement. He was a moving spirit in the organisation of the Northern Baptist Convention and the Federal Council of Churches, and he served terms as president of each. He devoted a great deal of energy to preparing materials on the Bible that would help modern people discover its relevance to the social situation of today. To this end he founded and edited journals and magazines and wrote literature for Sunday schools.

Much of the time Mathews wrote as though changes in doctrinal formulations and group practice do not affect a deeper level of Christian identity. He wrote, for example:

> Theology will change but Christian experience and faith will continue ... The great values which have been increasingly realized and expressed by successive theologians, reflecting successive social experiences, will continue to project themselves into the religious life of the future. They will give rise to new doctrines, as group interests change, but Christianity will breed true to itself because it will be developed by groups of Christians whose needs and satisfactions are of the same general type.[7]

But Mathews increasingly realised that he could not formulate an account of the experience and faith which continue in separation from the beliefs and practices which change. This led him to accept the more radical implications of his recognition of Christianity as a socio-historical movement. He stated that 'the only definition which can include the variations of the Christian movement is that Christianity is the religion of those who call themselves Christians ... Modern Christianity is the descendant of the religion of the men who wrote the New Testament, but, it is not identical with its ancestor'.[8] Although Mathews did think that those 'who have called themselves Christians have regarded Jesus as the author of their salvation',[9] the area of belief, including beliefs about Jesus, was left entirely relative.

The chief alternative Mathews saw to his own position was not orthodoxy, or even the Ritschlianism which flourished at the time, but rather philosophy of religion. He saw that modern people could seek through philosophy to arrive at religiously important beliefs. He wrote, 'there is involved here the ... profound choice between religion as a form of social behavior rationalized and directed by intelligence and religion as a philosophy in which the historical and social elements of an organized movement are to be ignored'. According to this choice, people 'who hold approximately the same religious convictions' develop markedly different attitudes.[10]

Although his own choice was clearly on the side of the historical approach, there were elements in his thought which paved the way for a marked shift in focus of the Chicago School. Although for him the primary context of religious life is social, he recognised also a cosmic dimension. Christianity must adjust its teachings to what we learn of the cosmos from the natural sciences. Mathews recognised that characteristic religious acts such as prayer and worship may not survive such admustment, but he saw no alternative to complete openness, and he personally found the implications of science supportive of the religious response.

Mathews's treatment of the doctrine of God reflects his dual concern with the social and the cosmic context. He wrote: 'All the various conceptions of the object of worship ... are relative to the conscious needs and the dominant social mindsets of various times and civilizations. The meaning of the word God is found in the history of its usage in religious behavior.' [11] However, this did not mean for Mathews that the object of worship is simply a human projection. He knew, what Tillich later pointed out, that 'projection always is projection *on* something'. [12] Mathews was convinced that the something in question was 'the personality-evolving and personally responsive elements of our cosmic environment with which we are organically related'. [13] That there are such elements, Mathews believed, is indicated as much by our modern knowledge as it has ever been. Hence the task now is to formulate conceptions of these forces appropriate to our social experience and need. The word 'God' refers to these conceptions rather than to the forces themselves or the scientific description of them.

Although interest in the personality-evolving forces of the cosmos did not shift Mathews's primary attention from sociology and history to natural science and philosophy, in principle it opened the way to a philosophical reflection about the personality-evolving forces that was informed by evolutionary science. Within the Chicago school this interest was represented chiefly by Gerald Birney Smith, who introduced students to the organismic thinking of such writers as Henri Bergson, Lloyd Morgan, Samuel Alexander, Jan Smuts and Alfred North Whitehead. The early writings of a young

American philosopher of religion, Henry Nelson Wieman, also caught the attention of both Smith and Mathews.

When Whitehead turned to religion in the Lowell Lectures of 1926, the Chicago faculty was keenly attentive to what he said. However, the book embodying those lectures, *Religion in the Making*,[14] disturbed them because of the strangeness of its language and conceptuality. Mathews invited Wieman, who was a visiting professor at McCormick Seminary in Chicago at the time, to come to the Divinity School to explain the book, and the success of the occasion confirmed Mathews's interest in him and led to the invitation to join the faculty. Wieman began teaching at Chicago in 1927 and continued until his retirement in 1947. In 1928 Charles Hartshorne joined the faculty of the Department of Philosophy. Their influence on the Divinity School community led to a shift of emphasis and dominated the second phase of the Chicago school. Because of the marked differences between them, and because what has come to be known as process theology is largely the result of their work, they are treated separately in the two following sections.

II

Wieman had attended the Presbyterian seminary at San Anselmo, California, and had studied in Germany under Eucken, Windelband and Troeltsch. However, he wrote that 'during these years' he 'was not aware of any further insight changing the structure' of his thought.[15] His major inspiration up to that time came from his reading of Bergson, an influence that coloured also the intellectual development of the years of his doctoral studies in philosophy at Harvard under Hocking and Perry. The other major influences were the writings of Dewey and Whitehead. Thus Wieman came to Chicago as a philosopher of religion, understanding the religious problem in the way over against which Mathews interpreted his own commitment to the Christian socio-historical movement.

But despite this difference, there was considerable continuity between Wieman and the older Chicago school. The socio-historical approach had always been pursued in continuity with empirical inquiries into human beings and religious experience, and the early Chicago school was quite open to the new discipline of psychology of religion and its relevance to religious education. Wieman was an empirical philosopher with strong psychological interests. The socio-historical concerns were also seen as broadly naturalistic in spirit. Wieman was a naturalist. Wieman shared with the earlier representatives of the Chicago school their complete rejection of all forms of supernaturalism and any bondage to past authority. The task was to think in the present with the tools now available to us and to be guided without reserve by the conclusions to which our thought brings us. In the understanding of the present situation Wieman opposed, just as strongly as the others, any introduction of a speculative element. The need is to limit our affirmations to that which can and must be accepted by any honest and open-minded person who looks at the facts we are now given. To associate Christian faith with any special claim upon intellectual assent is defeatist. Wieman agreed with Mathews that God could be identified in some way with the personality-producing forces in the universe, although he did not adopt this formulation as his own.

The points of difference, however, are not less striking. In the first place Wieman was no historian and rarely thought in historical categories. For him the avenue to religious truth lay in present experience and, at least during the earlier years, 'he dismissed historical study of the faith as having no resources for the present task'.[16] In the second place, Wieman was only incidentally concerned with sociology. For him the variety of social structures seemed secondary to the continuous reality of God's work in the world and man's participation therein. In the third place, Wieman turned attention away from human concepts and values to the reality of God as that which is of interest to the religious person. In the fourth place, whereas the older Chicago School had been exceedingly suspicious of mysticism, Wieman appealed to the sheer immediacy of the knowledge of God. It seemed to him necessary to distinguish the immediate 'acquaintance with' God of the religious person from the indirect 'knowledge about' to which at best scientific knowledge could lead.

The basis of these differences between the older Chicago school and Wieman lie in their different subject matters. Whereas the former had made religion, and specifically Christianity, the object of investigation, Wieman regarded God as such as the proper object of investigation. Our task, he insisted, is not to develop religious ideas suitable to our present social situation but to subject ourselves and our situation to the working of that reality which is God. Furthermore, this reality, far from being some dark, mysterious, and remote force, is known immediately by everyone. It is that upon which all that is good in human life depends, for it is that process in which human good comes to be. And this reality can be directly analysed and described.

The impact of Wieman in the American scene has sometimes been compared with that of Barth upon Continental theology,[17] and a parallel does exist at the point at which both men direct attention away from humanity and human values to the work of God which is understood as prior to and sovereign over human endeavors. But it must be equally apparent that Wieman was far removed from Barth and incapable of appreciating the latter's work. The sovereign reality to which Wieman calls attention is immediately knowable in everyone's experience. The question of whether authority can be ascribed to the Scriptures or to the Christ event is a secondary question to be discussed only after the essential understanding of God is achieved. Although religious knowledge is different from scientific knowledge in character, it is distinguished not by any appeal to historical revelation, but rather only by the greater immediacy of that reality which it empirically apprehends and describes.

Wieman's view is that what is of supreme importance is the growth of human good. By good he intends qualitative meaning or richness of integrated experience. Our concern should and must be to learn how the good grows. Wieman described in detail the creative process of interpersonal communication or interchange in which this occurs.[18] This process (which must be recognised as one among the many processes that make up the world) is not manipulable in relation to foreseen ends, for it is the process in which unforeseen and unforeseeable good emerges.

The human problem is that we all too often commit ourselves to particular past products of the creative event, that is, to particular values as embodied in ideas or institutions. These values are real values, but the effort to preserve them can easily work against the process that produced them and that can produce new goods. Commitment to such already-realised values is idolatry, and against such idolatry we must ever protest in the name of commitment to the creative event itself. This event Wieman understood to be God.

Although we cannot foresee the outcome of the creative process or bend it to our desires, we can learn how to produce conditions in which it can be freed for maximum effectiveness. This is possible only as we direct critical inquiry to empirical study both of the character of the process and of the circumstances of its effective working. To this inquiry, and to acting on its findings in all areas of life, Wieman devoted himself and called his students.

The objection is sometimes raised against the Chicago school that it is naively optimistic. It is true that most of the early faculty shared in the view that there had been progress in history and that Christians could expect that their aspirations for a better world were gradually being satisfied and might eventually be fulfilled. This optimism, however, was more a reflection of the temper of the times than a specific theological feature of the school. The socio-historical method is independent of this confidence. In any case, the later representatives of the Chicago school, beginning with Wieman, lacked this assurance about a better future. For them, possibilities not only of advance but also of decline, even of the destruction of the human species, lay before us. Their theology left the future radically open. Criticism of Wieman for not taking sin and evil with sufficient seriousness is based on a misunderstanding. The misunderstanding reflects a fundamentally different way of conceiving the relation of God and the world.

The usual formulations of the problem of evil arise out of this different matrix of ideas. Most Christians attribute to God the kind of power which implies that the world God created *should* be entirely, or at least fundamentally, good. When they encounter the actuality of suffering and injustice, the impurity of even the best motives, and the mutual destructiveness even of a relatively virtuous people, and when they discover also the depths of sin which erupt on a massive scale in human history from time to time, they are overwhelmed by the incongruity between what is and what, at some deep level, they feel *should* be the case. If they do not deny the reality of God altogether, or revolt against God, they are often led to engage in complex and convoluted dialectics to avoid declaring God, the sovereign of this world, to be evil.

This kind of struggle does not arise from the assumptions of Wieman's mature thought. There is no reason to expect the world as a whole to be characterised by goodness. Our knowledge of the world gained from science suggests that it is at best indifferent to human concerns. There are obviously many processes at work that are destructive, and there can be little doubt that the disappearance of the human species is simply a matter of time. What is perplexing is that there is any good at all. But there is, and this fact is awe-inspiring. Because there are so many destructive processes it becomes all the more important that we attend to that one process which is constructive, and that we relate ourselves to it in a way that will strengthen its working. This orientation will not eliminate suffering and injustice, but it can extend that limited sphere in which elements of joy and justice are to be found. In the end this, too, will disappear, but that is all the more reason to give ourselves to the creative process now.

To take this position is not to underestimate evil or to be naively optimistic. It does, however, lead to a preoccupation with good, whereas much of the best theology of the Christian tradition is preoccupied with evil. There is lacking in the Chicago school a subtle and profound analysis of evil such as may be found in the writings of Wieman's contemporary, Reinhold Niebuhr. It is this unfortunate lack that leads to the inaccurate criticisms of the school as unduly optimistic.

III

Charles Hartshorne joined the faculty of the University of Chicago in 1928, just one year after Wieman came. However, Hartshorne was a member of the department of philosophy and only gradually became influential in the Divinity School. From 1943, until he left Chicago in 1955, he held a joint appointment in the Philosophy Department and in the Divinity School. During those years he had a strong influence on some of those students who later became known as process theologians.

Hartshorne had been an assistant of Whitehead at Harvard, and he identified himself closely with Whitehead's philosophy. Nevertheless, Hartshorne was far along toward a philosophic position of his own before he came into contact with Whitehead. He had already been influenced by William Ernest Hocking and Charles Peirce, although these men's thoughts were also filtered through Hartshorne's own special interests and insights.[19]

Unlike Peirce and Whitehead, Hartshorne's central interests from the first centred on metaphysical questions and especially on the understanding of God. From early in his life he was convinced that the actuality of God as ideal and inclusive reality is immediately implied in all thought and experience and is therefore rationally certain. The problem is to get people to recognise what they already somehow know. For this reason, the ontological argument for the existence of God was for Hartshorne the most adequate rational expression of the necessity of God's existence. The problem for him was not so much the correctness of the argument but finding a way of formulating the argument that will compel recognition of its soundness.[20]

Hartshorne's conviction of the certainty of God's existence brought him into close relation with the earlier leaders of the Chicago school, but it functioned in a quite different way. These men had been convinced that belief in the field of religion must be formed by the same methods of inquiry that worked so well in the natural and social sciences. This was impossible so long as doubt existed with respect to the reality of the subject matter of the inquiry. Since 'God' identifies part of this subject matter, the word must be so defined as to remove the possibility of doubting the reality of that to which it refers. In this project they were remarkably successful. It would be difficult, for example, to doubt that there are personality-producing forces, or events of interpersonal interaction in which the lives of individuals are enriched. And that means that it would be difficult to doubt that 'God', in Mathews's or Wieman's sense has a real reference.

What Hartshorne means by God is in greater continuity with traditional Christian faith. But despite his own confidence that when the word 'God' is rightly understood the reality of its referent must be recognised as necessary, other people require a great deal of persuading. Even the ontological argument is an *argument*, and a very subtle and complex one at that. A great deal of intellectual activity is expended in demonstrating that the reality of God is given in and with all human experience and thought. And much of this activity is of a kind quite strange to the dominant currents of contemporary philosophy. Indeed, whereas the earlier Chicago school had set its face against any understanding of Christian faith that required defending disputable philosophic views, Hartshorne was engaged in creating a metaphysical position in lonely isolation from the prevailing mood of American philosophy. Thus, much of what had been opposed in the earlier Chicago school as speculative entered the school forcefully for the first time in the person of Hartshorne.

That in spite of this strangeness to the Chicago tradition Hartshorne was taken with utmost seriousness is a tribute to his personal stature and the quality of his mind. It also is an indication of a new mood in the Divinity School. The task was not so much to reformulate belief in a non-problematic way, but to construct a structure of belief in a situation in which everything, including the passion for social justice, was problematic. Furthermore, there was little effort to give direction to the churches. Rather, the primary concern was for a community of struggling faculty and students to find a place to stand for themselves. In such a situation the question was one of individual intellectual persuasion rather than of the acceptability of beliefs in a wider circle.

From an early point in his career Hartshorne was convinced of a fundamental perversity in the orthodox Christian theological position.[21] In continuity with Greek thought, Christian theologians have conceived God as perfect, and with this, Hartshorne fully concurred. It is the existence of perfection that he intended to show. But, also in continuity with Greek thought, theologians have conceived this perfection to be a timeless, changeless, absolute. Hartshorne believed that this understanding of perfection not only runs counter to the Biblical witness but also is philosophically destructive. In Hartshorne's view such a timeless, changeless absolute is always abstract. The concretely actual is temporal and in process. Hence the effort of theologians to affirm the actuality of the timeless and changeless has led to absurdities. These in their turn have led to the rejection of the idea of God in general. The ontological argument for the existence of God cannot prove the existence of something that is self-contradictory.[22] Because classical theism has committed itself to basic inconsistencies, no argument can establish its truth. The need is for a doctrine of God that is self-consistent and consistent also with our beliefs about the world.

Hartshorne's conviction that the Totality is perfect and, therefore, is God, is bound up with his panpsychism. He believes that every real individual is a unit of feeling, and that all feeling is feeling of other feelings. One of his earliest books is entitled *Beyond*

Humanism.[23] It is a sustained attack against all the ways in which human beings have set themselves up as the ultimate and inclusive reality. Against this he argues that animals also feel, and that as we descend the scale of organisms we find simpler and simpler feelings but never cross the line to units that do not feel at all. Similarly, when we ascend the scale we can go beyond ourselves to the universe as a whole, which is also a unit of feeling incomparably superior to us. Entities such as stones and plants, which do not themselves possess feelings, are made up of molecules and cells, which do. That most such feelings are not conscious in any ordinary sense of 'conscious' is no argument against this position.

The argument for such metaphysical claims cannot, of course, be empirical. They are rational, and of a style alien to the rest of the Chicago tradition. There is an appeal to intuition at some point, but the rational argument is that the doctrine of panpsychism can provide a superior comprehensive explanatory theory.

The claim is made clearly in *Beyond Humanism* and elaborated in great detail in subsequent books:

> It is the universal rule of scientific induction that a hypothesis must explain more than one set of facts. It is also a rule of philosophizing to systematize and solve problems by constant reference to other problems. Now the mind—body relation is one problem. There is also the problem of the subject—object relation. There is, third, the general problem of causal order in nature. Traditionally these three problems have been too often dealt with in isolation from one another. Moreover, there are still other related problems: the nature of time, the nature of individuality, the way in which one mind knows other minds. These six problems are open to a single solution. The name for this solution is 'organic sympathy',[24]

which Hartshorne elsewhere calls the feeling of feeling.

Just as our conscious human experience unconsciously feels the unconscious feelings of the cells of the brain and achieves a unity of its own life of feeling, so the Totality that is God feels our feelings in the unity of perfect experience. The divine feeling of the world is at once perfect knowledge and perfect love. This involves perfect passibility, perfect mutability and perfect relativity. These are the perfections that seem to Hartshorne most important. However, it is true that there is also something impassible, immutable, and absolute in God. That is God's essence. God changes not, in the sense that God is always and necessarily perfectly related to all things. But this changeless essence is abstract, whereas God in concreteness is constantly enriched by the new feelings derived from the contingent events in the world.

For Hartshorne this understanding of God is not only inspiring of worship and devotion but also the answer to the fundamental existential question. This question arises from our experience of temporality. The realisation of some value in a moment requires, in order to be seriously affirmed, the conviction that it matters beyond itself. Its sheer occurrence, if followed immediately by passage into total oblivion, would not be significant. Of course human memory preserves from such oblivion some of what happens, but this is only a partial and fragmentary solution to the problem. The time will come when human memory will disappear from the world. The whole course of human history will then be as nothing — if there be no memory other than human memory, if there be nothing to which we contribute besides human memory. But if God as the Totality includes us in the everlasting divine life, if we contribute literally all that we are to God and make a difference forever in the divine experience, then all that happens has ultimate importance. Belief in God is thus the ground of the meaningfulness of all human action and experience.[25]

IV

The term *process theology* came to be used during the third phase of the Chicago school, the phase led by students of Wieman and Hartshorne. The summary of their ideas above has been guided by the features of their thought which caught the imagination of another generation of theologians. This exaggerates a difference between them and the earlier socio-historical school. In particular, it understates the importance of the political in their thought.

The truth is that neither Wieman nor Hartshorne was oblivious to the social dimensions of salvation. Wieman was concerned to show what commitment to the source of human good would mean in institutional and national life as well as in personal life.[26] It would be false in his case to say that personal salvation is primary and social action its by-product. Salvation is God's work at all levels. Similarly for Hartshorne salvation is not limited to individuals or even to the human species. It is creation as a whole which is saved by God.

Social and political occurrences are as important in the shaping of the creation as are private or individual acts.

Nevertheless, regardless of their own intentions, Wieman and Hartshorne contributed to a shift from social views of salvation to more personal concerns. They abandoned the socio-historical approach which was committed to the primacy of social salvation and, although they were concerned for social salvation, they did not organise their thought around this goal. During the thirties and forties the Social Gospel had come under severe theological criticism. It was no longer widely influential in the church. Hence students did not bring this concern with them to the Divinity School in the same way as in the first part of the century. They were more often concerned with such questions as whether they could continue to be Christians with integrity or whether it was intellectually responsible to believe in God in any sense.

The social emphasis did not disappear, but the curricular tendency was to separate it from systematic theology. Theology dealt with God and, of course, with anthropology. Ethics dealt with the need for justice in society. By 1946 the split was officially recognised in the curriculum. Students who specialised in ethics were required to study systematic theology, and students in systematic theology were required to study ethics. But questions of social salvation were largely separated from what was called constructive theology.

The place of the social emphasis within the department of theology can be clarified by reference to three of Wieman's students who continued teaching in that department after his retirement: Bernard Meland, Bernard Loomer and Daniel Day Williams.

Meland studied with Wieman when the latter first came to Chicago, collaborated with him on a book on American philosophies of religion[27] during his years of teaching elsewhere, and returned to Chicago in 1945. His interests were literary, aesthetic and cultural, as well as religious. He responded enthusiastically to a mystical note in Wieman's earlier writings, an encouragement of sensitivity to the subtler nuances of experience. He parted ways with Wieman as the latter focused more rigorously on the empirical analysis of the creative event as a particular type of process. He preferred that theological formulations should remain exploratory and tentative, functioning to heighten awareness and make it more appreciative.

With these sensitivities he addressed himself to a reconstruction of liberal theology within the process idiom, particularly as conveyed through the writings of Whitehead and William James.

Although Meland's interests did not lead him to a merely individualistic view of religion or salvation, they did lead away from sociology as the major conversation partner of theology. Much of his work was in the theology of culture, and he interpreted Christian faith as a formative ingredient of that culture more than as an individual appropriation of saving truth. He dealt with such problems as the relation of human beings to nature, the encounter of East and West, higher education and the secularisation of Western culture. He was deeply concerned with the symbolic or mythic dimensions of human experience, thought and language as expressive of a depth that systematic and discursive theology and philosophy too easily obscure.

Bernard Loomer was a student of Wieman during Wieman's last years at Chicago. He became associate dean while still a student and succeeded to the deanship shortly after completing his graduate studies. His influence was not only through his teaching but also through his insistent efforts to create a community of open critical reflection in both the faculty and the student body.

Loomer was deeply influenced by Wieman's own position, but his studies with both Wieman and Hartshorne led him to Whitehead. In the fifties he began teaching Whitehead's philosophy systematically and rigorously, but later he became increasingly aware of his differences from Whitehead as well as from Wieman and developed in a more pantheistic direction. Throughtout these philosophical changes Loomer remained committed to basic anthropological insights learned from Reinhold Niebuhr. Indeed, the influence of Niebuhr has been the most consistent feature of his thought.

Daniel Day Williams took a master's degree at Chicago and then went to Union Theological Seminary. At Union he studied especially with Reinhold Niebuhr. From there he returned to Chicago Theological Seminary to teach. Soon thereafter the faculties of the Divinity School and Chicago Theological Seminary, along with the Unitarian and Disciples faculties, merged into the Federated Faculty. The influence of Wieman shaped Williams's most basic commitments, but his theological formulations were far more sensitive to the issues as they had been discussed in the historic heritage of the church. Also he was deeply appreciative of the work of his teacher at Union, Reinhold Niebuhr, and appropriated much of Niebuhr's thought while defending against him some features of the liberal tradition. As the years passed he studied Whitehead's philosophy with greater care, and his later theology expresses a full-orbed appropriation of Whiteheadian conceptuality.[28]

Williams wrestled with the implications of both liberal theology and Niebuhr's brilliant critique for political theory and for the correct understanding of the relation of Christian faith to political life. His distinctive contributions were informed by insights derived from Wieman and Whitehead. His conclusions were in many instances congenial with the ideas of contemporary political theology on these subjects. But his reflection on these topics was but one aspect of his whole theological work. His thought as a whole was not political.

The strong influence of Niebuhr among the Chicago theologians was supported by interest in his thought among the ethicists as well. Indeed, during the years following Wieman's retirement, Niebuhr was, alongside Wieman and Hartshorne, the major influence on the Chicago community. It is ironic that this influence failed to evoke a vigorous protest against the continuing drift toward more individualistic ways of understanding salvation. Yet this irony characterised the effect of Niebuhr's work elsewhere as well. He himself was emphatic that we cannot seek personal salvation in separation from the salvation of society from injustice. Yet he offered little hope for any lasting success in this latter task. Hence the impact of his thought was to elicit reflection about our existential condition as persons who are committed to a justice we have little hope of realising in more than provisional and temporary ways. In this perspective, questions about grace and righteousness take on new urgency. We see the need for realistic appraisals of what is possible and for willingness to engage in the quest for realisable social goals even at the cost of involvements that offend our moral sensibilities. Forgiveness acquires a deeper meaning. We become suspicious of our own motives and are driven to keener self-examination. Thus we become more concerned with what it means to be a Christian in this difficult context than with the social goal of a justice which always eludes us. The quest for salvation becomes personal. Moral and religious appeals to gird up our loins for crusades on behalf of the poor and oppressed tend to sound naive despite, and partly because of, their admirable intentions. The influence of Niebuhr on the Chicago school thus counted against ready acceptance of the message of political theology in the sixties despite the agreement of its concern for social salvation with Niebuhr's own convictions.

From the perspective of the present form of process theology, the most important development at Chicago during the late forties and especially in the fifties was the increasing attention to Whitehead's own work, and especially to *Process and Reality*, his Gifford lectures. I have already noted that Whitehead was respected by the faculty in the twenties and that he was an important influence on Wieman. Wieman mediated Whitehead's influence in the thirties, but he was offended by the speculative direction of Whitehead's thought in *Process and Reality* and more and more distinguished his position from it, turning in the end to a stance of harsh hostility.[29] Hartshorne's mediation of Whitehead's thought to the Divinity School grew during the forties, but it took time to separate his own ideas from those of Whitehead. Even in the late forties distinguishing Whitehead from Hartshorne was a difficult task, and much of *Process and Reality* still remained a closed book. Perhaps the sheer intellectual challenge posed by that book constituted a further distraction from the social and political understanding of theology characteristic of the early Chicago school.

Technical mastery of Whitehead's conceptuality provided powerful tools for both criticism and constructive work. Such mastery made it possible to see that the emphases of both Hartshorne and Wieman could be affirmed as 'Whiteheadian' despite their differences. There was little difficulty in appropriating much of what Niebuhr taught, as well, within a Whiteheadian framework. Hence, the adoption of Whitehead's conceptuality did not seem to be in conflict with what had been learned from other teachers. For the most part it operated at a different level.

It would have been quite possible to assimilate the socio-historical method also within a Whiteheadian context, and if this had been done, process theology would have been richer and more adequate. Unfortunately, by the fifties most of the advocates of that approach were retired and the necessary stimulus for this work was lacking. Indeed, the historical disciplines as a whole had gone their separate way, and process theology no longer had much connection with

Biblical studies. When process theologians undertook to recover their relation with Biblical studies, the influence of Rudolf Bultmann was in the ascendancy, and Schubert Ogden consummated a marriage of Hartshorne's metaphysics with Bultmann's existential theology.[30] Although most others did not go that far, there were few protests based on the de-emphasis of the social or political understanding of salvation that was entailed. Indeed, Ogden appeared to stand at the cutting edge of the Chicago school. Bultmann's thought, too, could be assimilated in Whiteheadian conceptuality, once it was freed from the remnant of mythology that appeared to be associated with his affirmation of a unique act of God in the cross and resurrection of Christ. Accordingly when the challenge of political theology was felt in the late sixties, it was addressed to process theologians, many of whom had largely cast their lot with an existential anthropology and doctrine of salvation.[31]

Nevertheless, process theologians have responded to this challenge, slowly but seriously. Ogden, for example, is moving beyond Bultmann in a manner strikingly reminiscent of Sölle's earlier formulations. He writes:

> Just as in Bultmann's analysis the question of belief and truth that theology now faces can be adequately answered only by way of radical demythologizing and existentialist interpretation, so it is now clear to me that what is required if theology is to deal satisfactorily with the issues of action and justice (which for many persons are even more urgent) is a theological method comprising thoroughgoing de-ideologizing and political interpretation.[32]

Exposition of Whitehead must be postponed to subsequent chapters. This chapter has indicated only how his philosophy has largely operated as a conceptuality which makes possible the assimilation of highly diverse ideas worked out by others into a coherent unity. This has been an important function, but the adoption of Whitehead in this mode has meant that much recent process theology has received its primary theological content from different sources at different times with insufficient critical reflection. It has been too much influenced by the concerns and ideas currently dominant and has too often failed to bring its own distinctive resources to bear upon our common personal and social dilemmas. It would be easy for a Whiteheadian to assimilate much of what political theologians are saying as well, and this, too, would be an enrichment of process theology. But this would not be a sufficient or appropriate response to political theology. This theology does not intend to contribute a set of ideas to be assimilated with others. It intends to redirect the theological enterprise. To indicate the direction in which political theology points us I have lifted up the phrase of Dorothee Sölle, 'the indivisible salvation of the whole world'. The appropriate response of process theology to the challenge of political theology is to reorient itself to the service of this goal. To do so does not mean to abandon its own distinctive perspective and resources but rather to employ them to this end. The following chapters are an attempt to clarify what is therein entailed through discussion with the German political theologians.

NOTES

1 John B. Cobb, Jr., *A Christian Natural Theology Based on the Thought of Alfred North Whitehead* (Philadelphia, Pa.: Westminster Press, 1965).

2 Walter Rauschenbusch, *A Theology for the Social Gospel* (Nashville, Tenn.: Abingdon Press, 1978), p. 1.

3 Dorothee Sölle, *Political Theology*, trans. John Shelley (Philadelphia, Pa.: Fortress Press, 1971), p. 1, quoting Dietrich Bonhoeffer, *Letters and Papers from Prison*, ed. Eberhard Bethge, trans. Reginald H. Fuller and Frank Clarke, 3rd English ed. (New York: MacMillan, 1967), p. 158.

4 Shirley Jackson Case, *The Evolution of Early Christianity: a Genetic Study of First Century Christianity in Relation to its Religious Environment* (Chicago, Ill.: University of Chicago Press, 1914), p. 14. Troeltsch continued his commitment to the religious *a priori* as late as 1912, but it is absent from *Der Historismus und seine Probleme* which appeared shortly after his death in 1923. See the discussion of this point in Benjamin A. Reist, *Toward a Theology of Involvement* (Philadelphia, Pa.: Westminster Press, 1966), pp. 169—97.

5 Shailer Mathews, *New Faith for Old* (New York: MacMillan, 1936), p. 42.

6 The fullest development of his position is in Shailer Mathews, 'Theology and the social mind', *The Biblical World* vol. XLVI No. 4 (October 1915), pp. 201—48.

7 Shailer Mathews, 'Theology from the point of view of social psychology', *Journal of Religion* vol. III No. 4 (July 1923), pp. 350—1.

8 Shailer Mathews, *Is God Emeritus?* (New York: MacMillan, 1940), p. 71.

9 *Ibid.*

10   Mathews, *New Faith for Old*, p. 70.

11   Shailer Mathews, *The Growth of the Idea of God* (New York: Mac-Millan, 1931), p. 210.

12   Paul Tillich, *Systematic Theology*, vol. 1 (Chicago, Ill.: University of Chicago Press, 1963), p. 212.

13   Mathews, *The Growth of the Idea of God*, p. 226.

14   Alfred North Whitehead, *Religion in the Making* (New York: Mac-Millan, 1926).

15   Henry Nelson Wieman, 'Intellectual biography', *The Empirical Theology of Henry Nelson Wieman*, ed. Robert W. Bretall, Library of Living Theology, vol. 4 (New York: MacMillan, 1963), p. 7.

16   An unpublished letter to me from Bernard Meland.

17   Bernard E. Meland, 'A long look at the Divinity School and its present crisis', *Criterion*, vol. 1, No. 2 (summer 1963), p. 25.

18   See Henry Nelson Wieman, *The Source of Human Good* (Chicago, Ill.: University of Chicago Press, 1946), esp. pp. 58–69.

19   'Comment by Professor Charles Hartshorne' in Eugene H. Peters, *The Creative Advance* (St Louis, Mo.: Bethany Press, 1966), pp. 133–4.

20   His fullest treatment is in Charles Hartshorne, *The Logic of Perfection and Other Essays in Neoclassical Metaphysics* (LaSalle, Ill.: Open Court Publishing Company, 1962), pp. 2–117.

21   See for example, 'Two strands in historical theology', chapter III of Charles Hartshorne, *Man's Vision of God* (New York: Harper, 1941).

22   Charles Hartshorne, *The Logic of Perfection*, pp. 24–6.

23   Charles Hartshorne, *Beyond Humanism: Essays in the Philosophy of Nature* (Chicago, Ill.: Willett Clark & Co., 1937).

24   *Ibid.*, p. 195.

25   This point is richly developed by Hartshorne's student Schubert Ogden, 'The reality of God', in *The Reality of God and Other Essays* (New York: Harper and Row, 1963).

26   Henry Nelson Wieman, *The Directive in History* (Boston, Mass.: Beacon Press, 1949); *Man's Ultimate Commitment* (Carbondale, Ill.: Southern Illinois University Press, 1958); *Intellectual Foundations of Faith* (New York: Philosophical Library, 1961).

27   Henry Nelson Wieman and Bernard Meland, *American Philosophies of Religion* (Chicago, Ill.: Willett Clark & Co., 1936).

28   Daniel Day Williams, *The Spirit and the Forms of Love* (New York: Harper Philosophical Library, 1961).

29   Henry Nelson Wieman, *Intellectual Foundations of Faith* (New York: Philosophical Library, 1961).

30   Schubert Ogden, *Christ Without Myth: a Study Based on the Theology of Rudolf Bultmann* (New York: Harper, 1961) and *The Reality of God* (New York: Harper and Row, 1964). See also Ogden, 'Zur Frege der "richtigen Philosophie"', *Zeitschrift für Theologie und*

Kirche (1964), pp. 103–124. Under the influence of liberation theologies Ogden has subsequently recognised the one-sidedness of these formulations. In 1978 he wrote about *Christ Without Myth*: 'The newer theological developments of the past decade, especially the emergence of the various theologians of liberation, compelled the conclusion that the most urgent theological problem today, at any rate for the vast number of persons who still do not share in the benefits of modernity, is a problem more of action and justice than of belief and truth. Perhaps nothing dates — and severely limits — the argument of my book quite so much as the global way in which I there spoke of "modern man" and of "the theological problem", without taking sufficient account of the vast differences between the rich nations and the poor nations, and all the other differences — racial and sexual as well as economic and cultural — by which persons even in our own society remain divided.' Schubert M. Ogden, 'An outline still to be filled out', *The Christian Century* (17 May 1978), pp. 538–9.

31 Despite the attraction of existentialist philosophy and theology to process theologians during the sixties the major senior representatives of the movement continued to give attention to public issues in portions of their books. See for example, Henry Nelson Wieman, *The Intellectual Foundations of Faith* (New York: Philosophical Library, 1961); Charles Hartshorne, *The Logic of Perfection and Other Essays in Neoclassical Metaphysics* (La Salle, Ill.: Open Court, 1962); Bernard E. Meland, *The Realities of Faith: the Revolution of Cultural Forces* (New York: Oxford University Press, 1962); and Daniel Day Williams, *The Spirit and the Forms of Love* (New York: Harper & Row, 1968). For contributions of process theology to discussion of public issues in the seventies see Note 1 to the Preface.

32 'Faith and freedom', *The Christian Century* (17 Dec. 1980), pp. 1241–2.

Chapter Three

THEOLOGICAL METHOD IN A
POLITICAL PROCESS THEOLOGY

Thus far I have simply described two traditions which developed quite independently of each other. My interest, however, as a process theologian is to show how process theology can become a political theology committed to the indivisible salvation of the whole world. This, of course, does not mean becoming a disciple of Metz, Moltmann or Sölle. It does not entail adopting a theological position derived from criticism of transcendental Thomism, of Barth or of Bultmann. It requires, instead, the transformation of the tradition sketched in the preceding chapter into a political theology in the sense that it must become committed to the indivisible salvation of the whole world.

Any political theology must be characterised both by appropriate methods and by appropriate doctrines. Process theology has resources that should prove useful. They differ, however, from those that have been drawn upon in existing forms of political theology. In this chapter methodological approaches employed by Metz, Moltmann and Sölle will be critically appraised, modified and appropriated from the perspective of process thought. In Chapter Four some of the doctrines of process theology will be proposed as alternative or supplementary to dominant German formulations. The thesis is that although the resultant theology differs from what is now called political theology it would not for that reason have less claim to the term.

There are differences in the methods of the three German theologians, but there are some themes sufficiently important to all three to demand careful study. One is political hermeneutic. All three understand political theology at least in part as political interpretation of the gospel. A second is memory. Metz, at length, and Moltmann, occasionally, interpret Christianity and its political practice in terms of memory. A third is praxis. All agree that there can be no authentic Christian theology apart from political practice. These themes are interconnected, but it will be convenient here to treat them in the separate sections of this chapter.

I

All three theologians emphasise hermeneutic as central to the task of political theology. This is not surprising. Some concern for hermeneutic is universal, and in Barthian, Bultmannian and especially post-Bultmannian theology hermeneutic has been the *central* concern. It is not surprising that it should be the post-Bultmannian, Dorothee Sölle, who develops the case for a political hermeneutic most clearly, since it has been the Bultmannians who have discussed the topic most fully. Hermeneutic means interpretation, and for the Bultmannians, what is chiefly to be interpreted is the Bible. Sölle is quite Bultmannian in her view that the task of theology is to interpret the Gospel, and that the task of political theology is to give a political interpretation of the Gospel.

This definition of the theological task is quite different from that of process theology. Process theology has understood its responsibility more as that of clarifying what a Christian in the modern world should affirm and of guiding the church toward appropriate formulations of its faith. Of course, process theology cannot fulfil this responsibility without interpreting Scripture, and the separation of process theology in recent decades from the close involvement in Biblical scholarship of the earlier Chicago school has led to critical weaknesses which are only now being addressed.[1] Nevertheless, for process theology the appropriate relationship to the Bible can not be exhausted by hermeneutic.

This difference is connected with differences in the way theology is related to preaching. In central Europe it sometimes seems that the deepest reason for preserving and developing the theological tradition in the university has been that a profession exists whose chief function is the proclamation of the Biblical message. Since the mere recitation of Biblical passages does not suffice, these professionals require guidance as to how to move from text to sermon. It has been the task of theologians to provide such guidance.

The problem is that much of what is found in the text can not and should not be proclaimed today as the truth by which Christians are to live. If we ask of the text what opinions it reflects with respect to cosmology, it is clear that honest answers would often include beliefs that can not be recommended to contemporary congregations. Hence there must be some process whereby an appropriate message is elicited from texts much of whose content is irrelevant or even erroneous.

No one within the hermeneutical tradition has stated the problem more clearly than Bultmann or provided a more influential answer. Bultmann teaches that the correct question to ask of the text is the existential question, that is, the understanding of existence it expresses. Heidegger has clarified for us what that question means, and with his aid we can find in all religious texts answers that challenge us with respect to our own understanding of existence. The preacher's task is to confront us with the distinctively Christian understanding of existence as that is found in the New Testament.

Sölle rejects this view.[2] The sermon is not for her so central. The text is interpreted for the sake of the indivisible salvation of the whole world. The sermon is only one way in which this end can be served.

As a political theologian Sölle modifies the Bultmannian theory of interpretation in another way as well. In Chapter One we noted her critique of existential interpretation. Form critical study recognises, and indeed emphasises, the socio-historical context in which the text functioned in the early church. It emphasises its public function. But when Bultmann turned to the analysis of the pre-understanding with which the hearer now comes to the text, he ignored the socio-historical situation and spoke instead of the existential historicity of the hearer. Sölle insists that our preunderstanding must recognise our political situation as well as that of the text in its original use. Both of these shifts bring her hermeneutic into closer relation with process theology.

In other respects, however, Sölle brings to political theology features of Bultmann's hermeneutic which do not fit well with process theology. For Bultmann criticism is applied to every verbal formulation of the kerygma. No doctrine stands beyond criticism.

But all this criticism is in the service of the kerygma itself. That does stand beyond criticism. Sölle criticises Bultmann for turning from Jesus to the witness to Jesus's death and resurrection in his search for the kerygma. But on the formal point she stands with him. She writes:

> The kerygma ... as address, claim, or — as I would interpret it with a non-Bultmannian expression — the 'absolute' in Christian faith, is not subject to criticism. The liberation that love engenders and the claim that it lays upon us are absolutely binding; they are kerygmatic address, which, as Bultmann interprets Paul, 'accosts each individual, throwing the person himself into question by rendering his self-understanding problematic, and demanding a decision of him.' The kerygma can be defined as 'absolute' in two respects. First, it is unsurpassable, for no one can promise, give, or demand more than love; second it is underivable, for it cannot be grounded within the world.[3]

Sölle's formulation of the Biblical absolute is a moving one, but from the point of view of process theology insistence on an absolute creates problems. The history of constantly changing formulations of the Biblical absolute suggests that we need a critical study of how each one fits the needs of those who formulate it. There is no reason to think that in Sölle this history has finally come to an end.

Shirley Jackson Case clearly saw the negative consequences of the search for an absolute or essence in the Bible. He wrote in 1914:

> Any effort to fix upon an irreducible minimum or genuine 'essence' can succeed only by setting up some quantity of experience, or belief, or practice as essential, while all other features are denominated unessential. But this is a doubtful procedure. In the first place, instead of defining Christianity comprehensively, attention is centred upon certain restricted phases of the whole. Even if it were possible to ascertain with perfect certainty a given sum of items possessed in common by all Christians, it would still be quite unfair to neglect all other features which may have been equally important and essential at certain periods and within particular circles. To affirm, for example, that the essential elements of Christianity in the first century were only those items which believers of that day have in common with the 'liberal' theologian of the twentieth century, is to eliminate as unessential to first-century believers their realistic eschatology, their belief in demons and angels, their vivid supernaturalism,

their sacramentalism, their notion of the miraculous content of religious experience, and various other features of similar importance. Certainly primitive Christianity cannot be perfectly understood without taking full account of all these items, and one may fairly question the legitimacy of any interpretation which does not make them even 'essential' to Christianity's existence in the first century.[4]

Of course, all this can be affirmed as 'essential' for first-century Christianity only when we adopt a truly historical understanding. In such an understanding we can see the living whole of a faith as indivisible into a kernel and husk. But we can also see that this living whole, in so far as it is truly living, is in constant change. No portion of it is immune to such change. Some portions may remain relatively unchanged while others alter drastically, but there can be no predetermination of what will change and how much. The question is not whether there will be changes but whether these changes are responsible developments in response to new challenges. Sölle is rightly calling for a change today toward a fuller recognition of the political character and calling of the Christian community. Those who developed the socio-historical method shared her view. They agreed with her that there is much in the Bible, and specifically in Jesus, which points in that direction. They did not, however, see a need to absolutise anything in the Bible as a final standard of judgement, even what Sölle calls the gospel's 'nonderivable promise and the demand for peace, freedom, and justice for all people'.[5] The test of our present judgements is not their conformation to any Christian absolute but rather whether they have developed responsibly through Christian history. How we are today to address oppressive social systems is not to be decided by an appeal to a Biblical absolute but by our shared reflection on what we are now called to do as Christians. Of course that reflection will be attentive to our whole history and especially to the early stages of our movement. The prophets, Jesus, Paul, John and many others have great authority for us today. But there is no one locus of *absolute* authority. Our concern is faithfulness to God's call today, and we can be guided in that faithfulness by many authorities. Finally *we* must decide.

From the perspective of process theology a truly critical and a truly political theology must learn to do without absolutes. In fact, such an absolute does not seem necessary for Sölle. Her call for service of the indivisible salvation of all the world rings true quite apart from the appeal to an absolute. It is for *us now* the claim of our faith. That it has not always been the appropriate formulation does not reduce its force today.

Sölle accepts also from Bultmann the analysis of the hermeneutical situation. She thinks of a text to be studied and a preunderstanding which we bring to that text. For Bultmann this preunderstanding is brought to all the New Testament texts, and they are all to yield the Christian understanding of existence.

There are problems with this type of procedure even for existential hermeneutics, as Bultmann acknowledged in passing.[6] Not every New Testament passage expresses the truly Christian understanding of existence. But the problem is far more acute for political hermeneutic. For it is not clear that all, or even most, New Testament texts express an appropriate political understanding. For Bultmann an understanding of existence is something we bring with us to the text as well as something we find expressed there. The one we bring is brought into question by the one we find. Sölle recognises that in a political hermeneutic the burden falls upon the preunderstanding of the one who approaches the text. It is there that the understanding of the importance of political structures is to be found and also the conviction that they are subject to change and that through changing them the human condition can be improved. One does not find these views in the texts, even in Jesus. Sölle writes:

> In the hermeneutical process this contemporary preunderstanding that structures can be transformed is confronted by the gospel and thereby is criticized, modified, and liberated, but not by any means simply negated. It is within this hermeneutical process that the question about Jesus' relation to the transformation of this world must be reformulated. Even if we deny that Jesus worked for transformation in the explicit sense of deriving the dialectic of individual and society from social structures, or beginning the process of transformation with changes in property and social relationships, it cannot be overlooked that in an indirect sense, the manner in which Jesus thought and acted *de facto* broke open and transformed the social structures of the world in which he lived.[7]

It seems that Sölle herself recognises that the appeal is not to the texts but to the history. It is not what Jesus intended or said or what the texts assert, but the actual consequences in history which are her touchstone.

As a sensitive participant in the contemporary situation she is convinced that Christians should be involved in righting the social wrongs that degrade so much of humankind. She is rightly convinced also that her conviction has deep roots in the Bible and especially in Jesus's concern for the poor and oppressed. She does not intend to subject this conviction to the outcome of research about Jesus's political activity. She holds that 'it is meaningless to ask: Was Jesus a revolutionary? Where did he stand on violence, on landed property? Instead, we as his friends who affirm the intention of his decision must attempt for our part to declare where we stand today on revolution, property, or violence. This function of his on our behalf (his *beneficia*) is more important than the words and deeds discoverable by the historian, which lead only to imitation, not to discipleship'.[8]

All of this breaks out of the categories of Bultmann's hermeneutic which is limited to the preunderstanding we bring and the understanding we find in the text. But because Sölle still tries to use this structure, she does not go far toward liberating herself from Bultmann's pattern of thinking. The direction of her own thought would lead to viewing what she calls the preunderstanding as itself the appropriate historical outcome of Jesus's work. But by calling it a preunderstanding she assimilates it to the idea that it arises in an autonomous modern world and then becomes our special basis for questioning Jesus. Yet she does not seriously intend to subject her preunderstanding to possible rejection from the side of Jesus, nor does she find an understanding on Jesus's part which challenges it. This opens her to the charge that her basic commitments are not Christian, whereas she knows that in fact they are. The hermeneutical structure she adopts undercuts the valid point she wants to make.

Sölle's real self-understanding could gain better expression in the forms offered by the socio-historical school. She sees a socio-historical movement described and reflected in the Bible. She sees Jesus as having given a decisive formulation which has had profound historical influence. She sees herself and others as living from that influence in a new socio-historical situation which calls for different actions. She knows that she cannot find the message for today's situation in the language of one who lived in another situation, but she is confident that what she is saying and doing is in faithful continuity with what Jesus said and did. Her claim should not be then that she is being obedient to a timeless absolute which has just been discovered. It should be that she is faithfully discerning the responsible actions of that movement which arose through the long history of Biblical times and which is alive today.

This perspective would not undercut the importance of interpreting the Scriptures. It would frankly recognise that different parts of the Bible have differentiated importance in changing socio-historical circumstances. Sometimes it is Jesus, sometimes Paul, sometimes John and sometimes the Old Testament prophets who speak the word that proves most illuminating. The theological task is not only to interpret given texts, but also to find the texts that are relevant in different times and places. When a community seeks guidance it must turn to its history. There is no understanding of who we are in the present except through such study. The roots and origins of a movement are particularly important for its self-understanding. Sometimes past incidents or texts can be found to which it seems eminently appropriate to conform. But generally the relation is not like that. The authority of the past is looser, more fluid, more subject to our creative selection.

Such a view of the hermeneutical task is a fully political one. It carries the historical critical approach to its full conclusion, while supporting a partisan stance. We study our scriptures as participants in the Christian movement seeking to respond faithfully to the challenges of our time. Our identity depends on our rootedness. But a healthy identity depends on our willingness to confess the many crimes which our movement has committed. We find direction in the present as much by studying our past errors as by finding inspiration in those occasions when our ancestors in the faith used their freedom wisely.

II

The difficulty of establishing any absolute content for Christian faith has been widely recognised in modern Protestant thought. Accordingly, as Metz notes, Protestant theologians 'interpret faith above all as an act of faith, as *fides qua creditur*, as far as possible without any content'.[9] But a faith without content, Metz sees, 'is always in danger of obscuring the power of Christian faith, which is derived from its content and conviction, to criticize society'.[10] Metz finds no solution to this problem at the level of argumentative theology alone. He calls instead for an understanding of faith as memory.

> On the other hand, as *memoria*, faith makes it clear that Christian faith is a dogmatic faith which is tied to a certain content, a *fides quae creditur*. It also shows how it is able, because of this, to achieve the critical freedom which is related to the history of social freedom ... The Biblical traditions and the doctrinal and confessional formulae that are derived from these traditions appear in the light of this interpretation as formulae of *memoria*. In other words, they are interpreted as formulae in which the claim of promises made and past hopes and fears that have been experienced are recollected in the memory in order to break the grip of the prevailing consciousness, to obtain release from the compulsions and restrictions of the world today and to break through the banality of the present and the immediate future.[11]

Faith as memory is thus a powerful force in the present. It comes alive as ' ... dangerous remembrances, remembrances of hope and terror which were experienced and then were suppressed or silenced, which suddenly break through again into our one-dimensional everyday world ... There are remembrances with which we must reckon, remembrances, so to say, with future content, remembrances which do not deceptively relieve our burden ... Such remembrances are like dangerous and incalculable visitations out of the past ... Such remembrances press us to change ourselves in accordance with them.'[12]

Such memory has a narrative structure. That is, what is remembered are events ordered as stories. Narrative is not a primitive mode of knowledge that has been superseded by science nor a mere appendage to scientific thought. Instead it corresponds most fundamentally with our actual experience and shapes our identity. In particular, narrative memory shapes our identity as Christians. 'The intelligibility of Christianity cannot be transmitted theologically in a purely speculative way. It can only be transmitted in narrative – as a narrative and practical Christianity.'[13]

Metz is not asking for an end of argument in theology. Indeed, he himself engages extensively in argument. His objection is that argument has excluded narrative from theology and even from pastoral care, whereas without narrative as a way of shaping memory the power of Christianity to form our identity will be lost.

All this makes excellent sense from the perspective of process theology. Metz recognises Christianity as a movement constituted by a living identity with Jesus.[14] The socio-historical approach would prefer to speak of a movement constituted by living continuity with Jesus, but for it, too, this continuity would constitute its Christian identity. Such a movement cannot be defined by unchanging beliefs or structures, yet it can never exist apart from a content of faith. This content has its continuity with Jesus through the influence of Jesus, and that means primarily, although not exclusively, the memory of Jesus.

Metz writes of memory in general terms that are applicable to all. But for him the memory of Jesus is not simply one memory among others. It is the unique memory constitutive of Christian faith. Jesus is the incarnation of the God who is our future.

From the point of view of the socio-historical approach, Metz seems to separate Jesus too much from the larger story. Crucial though Jesus's role is, the memories by which the Christian community lives and maintains its identity include the stories of the first believers, the early church, and on down to our time. They go back before Jesus also through the history of Israel. When this memory of a rich and complex history is collapsed into the memory of Jesus and especially Jesus's passion, there is too much likelihood that the ever present Christian tendency to anti-Judaism will not be checked. Whereas Metz focuses on the passion of Jesus, process theology would want to point to the power and relevance, at different times and places, of the Exodus, the Jewish prophets, the resurrection and the conversion of Paul. One advantage of the narrative form is that we do not have to fix on one story told in one way at all times and places. We have a wealth of stories to draw upon without the need to relate them all systematically.

Process theology accentuates, even more than Metz does, the primacy of memory in the establishment of human identity. In the fullest sense I am now constituted by what I have been. If I tell someone who I am by offering categories under which I fit, I may be accurate. I am a male, married, a teacher, a Protestant and so forth. But this does not get at my personal identity. That identity I can share and express only by telling the story of my life. I *am* the continuation of that story, and as Metz stresses, my anticipations of the future are another expression of my memory of the past.

A part of my story includes my various efforts to reason, to speculate, to construct systems. Those efforts cannot be understood apart from my story, but from the point of view of process thought they can express a measure of transcendence of personal experience. Those efforts and their consequences affect the ongoing story. It is hard to tell how far Metz will go in accepting this positive role for speculative thought. But there is no apparent reason for excluding it from a political theology as long as its socio-historical grounding and political meaning are not neglected.

Much of what Metz says about memory and narrative resonates with what process theology has learned from H. Richard Niebuhr's classic work on *The Meaning of Revelation*.[15] There is, however, a certain difference. Niebuhr develops his approach to the confessing of our several stories as a way of accepting and even internalising pluralism. Metz is critical of the acceptance of pluralism, for he sees that it can turn the question of truth simply into the question of viewpoints. Respect for truth requires that 'any given theological position must strive to appropriate precisely those elements which other positions see as lacking or neglected in it'.[16] This seems a fine suggestion as far as it goes. Indeed, this book is written in order that process theology may appropriate some of those elements which political theologians have rightly shown to be lacking in it. But Metz could have deepened his response to pluralism through his emphasis on memory.

H. Richard Niebuhr pointed out that it is not enough for two communities to accept one another's beliefs. If they live by different memories, they will still remain external to one another. Protestants and Catholics can truly grow together only as they appropriate one another's memories of the period of their separation. The Council of Trent must become a part of the inner history of Protestants, and Luther and the Anabaptists must become part of the inner history of Catholics. If so, whatever happens at the level of institutions, Protestants and Catholics will be restored to a common Christian identity.

It is not clear whether Metz would agree to this particular extension of his discussion of memory. But he explicitly rejects this approach to other religious traditions, and he claims that his narrative theology enables him to avoid it. 'Narrative and practical Christianity can, in its encounter with ... other religions, keep hold of its eschatological and universal history of meaning without at the same time having to accept the histories of the other religions in a totality of meaning.'[17]

Process theology does not anticipate any totality of meaning. There will be no end at which all meaning is gathered together, and certainly this is impossible during the course of history. But meaning can be enlarged, and with it there can be an enlargement of identity. Metz himself illustrates this strongly in one dimension. His identity is not simply German or European but globally human. Yet in the face of the other religions he draws back.

It may be that this is based on too limited a model of narrative. There are, of course, simple linear narratives in which only one event takes place at a time. Hegel's narrative of the world Spirit presented it in such a linear form, and Teilhard's narrative of the development of life and humanity on this planet is also quite linear. But to tell even my own story well, I must break out of this linear mould. I cannot explain what happened in my life without speaking of the others who contributed to it. Events in my life are the result of converging forces often from several important sources. When I join a new movement, the memory of the history of that movement gradually becomes part of me. We must not confuse the 'cognitive primacy of narrated memory'[18] with a purely linear structure of memory. Metz's own stress upon the social constitution of the individual should overcome the tendency to think of narrative in linear terms.

If we recognise that our identity is richer as it is co-constituted by more strands of memory, then we will not want to use the narrative approach to the understanding of Christianity to close ourselves to other traditions whether religious or secular. Indeed our memories of our own Christian tradition will show us how extensively we have already assimilated other histories into our Christian memory, especially the history of Greco-Roman civilisation. Plato and Cicero are parts of our remembered history as well as Abraham and Moses. This is an enrichment of our identity, even, specifically, our Christian identity. We are enlightened as Christians also by our memory of Darwin, of Marx and of Freud. Our identity will not be impoverished if some day we incorporate also Gautama and Nagarjuna, Rabbi Hillel and Maimonides, into the remembered narrative by which we live.

The issue is not between process theology and political theology, but as to just how political theology is to be developed. There is much that Metz says about memory and narrative with which a process theologian can enthusiastically agree. Against the view that only by finding the meaning of the whole of history can meaning be given to life within it, we can agree with Metz in his quest for a meaning that is 'evoked, remembered and narrated (for all men) as a practical experience in the middle of our historical life'.[19] The importance, even the primacy, of suffering in our shared memory and its stimulus to free action are insights to be appropriated. But there is a tendency to exclude from Christian appreciation and appropriation experience and memory that could enrich us and add to our ability to attain solidarity with human beings who live with quite different meanings. That seems, from the perspective of process theology, to be a limitation to be overcome in the further development of political theology.

III

For political theology, practice is even more central to theological method than hermeneutic and narrative memory. This is clear in each of the three German theologians here discussed.

For Metz the primary problem of Christianity today is not that its doctrines are unclear or out of contact with current scientific and philosophical thought, but that its practice is not faithful. This is not a problem only in relation to external critics of Christianity but among Christians as well. 'What we have here is a deep suspicion, rooted in the pre-rational Christian consciousness, that the living identity of the Christian body with Jesus has become lost in later Christianity, that Christianity cast off its conformity to Christ a long time ago and that many of Jesus' intentions were long ago successfully taken over by other historical movements.'[20] Accordingly, 'the so-called historical crisis of identity is not a crisis of the contents of faith, but rather a crisis of the Christian subjects and institutions which deny themselves the practical meaning of those contents, the imitation of Christ'.[21] It is this conviction that leads Metz to call for 'a practical fundamental theology'.

Metz's practical fundamental theology 'is a theology that operates subject to the primacy of praxis'.[22] This practice is informed by memory which leads to the imitation of Christ. It is in the context of this imitation that Christological theories have their place and meaning. The praxis is social and political. For example, Metz writes, 'The forms of behaviour such as metanoia, exodus and the imitation of Christ which are constitutive in my idea of God and Christological and eschatological knowledge in general have a social and political structure'.[23] This is further explained: 'In this freedom of memory, the history of men as subjects in the presence of God is evoked and Christians are compelled to respond to the practical challenge of this history. In its praxis what will emerge, at least partially, is that all men are called to be subjects in the presence of God.'[24]

The influence of Bloch led Moltmann to reflections on Marx and to the incorporation of Marxist insights about the relation of theory and practice into his thought. Of particular importance is the famous eleventh thesis against Feuerbach: 'The philosophers have only *interpreted* the world in various ways; the point, however, is to *change* it.'[25] Bloch believed that 'the ultimate, enduring insight of Marx is that truth does not exist for its own sake but implies emancipation, and an interpretation of the world which has the transformation of the world as its goal and meaning, providing a key in theory and leverage in practice'.[26] Drawing on this tradition Moltmann writes that unless truth 'contains initiative for the transformation of the world, it becomes a myth of the existing world. Because reality has become historical and man experiences himself as a historical being, he will find a possible conformity of consciousness and existence only in historical practice. This is the event of truth'.[27]

Dorothee Sölle is not less committed to practice. The political hermeneutic of the gospel is for the sake of the salvation of the whole world. It makes the meaning of the gospel concrete in terms of some aspect of the contemporary political situation. It assumes the possibility of free action for the change of social institutions and awakens and directs that freedom. Political theology 'grasps the relation to truth no longer as one of contemplation and theory only, as accords with the Greek mind, but as an operative and practical relation'.[28] Sölle quotes Habermas: 'The unity of theory and praxis signifies the truth that is to be established and, conjointly, the supreme standard of reason, since within the situation of alienation all efforts that move toward the establishment of truth are already seen as rational. Reason is the entry into future truth.'[29] For Sölle it would be better to say: 'Faith is the entry into future truth.'[30] But the main point is that the truth to which we are committed is one that is not already realised. Our interpretation of the gospel is for the sake of its realisation. 'The verification principle of every theological statement is the praxis that it enables in the future.'[31]

The commitments Sölle expresses here led her more and more into a Marxist hermeneutic of the gospel. For example, the Marxist analysis of alienation provides her with a way of understanding Paul's doctrine of sin in Romans 1:23. This doctrine makes sense for her when we understand the power of sin under which we live as 'the power of produced things which dominates humans'.[32] Such an understanding empowers and directs practice appropriately.

None of these theologians believes that the practice of faith can be derived from political theology alone. Other disciplines must provide help in the analysis of the concrete situation within which Christians are called to act. Sölle recognises that this is not well developed, but she writes that in its entry into future truth 'theoretically at least, theology cooperates with other disciplines'.[33] Metz has moved from the recognition of the need for interdisciplinary co-operation to devoting extensive time and effort to its realisation. He has worked with Trutz Rendtdorff for the establishment at the University of Bielefeld of a permanent institute for bi-confessional theology in an interdisciplinary context. Already in 1970 the planning was far advanced and a conference was held to reflect on the project.[34] All that is lacking is the agreement of the Protestant and Catholic churches.

As explained in the preceding chapter, at the time that political theology arose in Germany, process theology in the United States was at its furthest removed from a praxis orientation. Although its interest in a credible doctrine of God and God's work in the world was grounded in existential and ultimately practical concerns, the relation to practice was little and poorly articulated. Although the situation has improved somewhat since then, recent process theology has still done little to clarify the relation between theory and practice.

When process theology does reflect on this central question, it finds it can learn much from the sources on which political theology draws. The situation as perceived from the point of view of process philosophy is one in which all thinking is done in a concrete, socially determined situation and expresses the interests which have arisen in that situation. Everyone is involved in practice before reflecting. From Marxism process theology can learn the importance of critical analysis of the interests that arise within the situation and of the way that the social situation controls thinking which does not become self-critical. It can seek to direct practice in terms of such critical self-understanding and to engage in theoretical reflection which is needed for the improved direction of practice. For process theology to develop in this way would be a great gain.

Nevertheless, process theology can never adopt this praxis model for theology without qualification.[35] Political theologians are right to warn Christians against the temptation to be drawn into abstract thought for its own sake in a world characterised by starvation and oppression, and thought that lacks relevance to the salvation of the whole world is a luxury the world cannot afford. But there is a danger that the call for relevance may be too short-sighted. Whitehead has shown us the powerful effects over two millenia of Plato's doctrine of the soul, especially as it was combined with Biblical ideas.[36] The relevance of his thought, judged by immediate consequences, was all too limited. But few political actions have contributed nearly as much to the salvation of the whole world. Theologians, of all people, should not underestimate the importance of great beliefs.

There is another limitation of that thought and practice which operate strictly within the praxis model. Practice is always theory-laden, and the relevance for which this model calls is relevance to a situation which is already perceived through established concepts. Action can lead to the correction of theory and the reconceptualisation of the situation and the praxis model calls for critical examination of goals. But there are limits as to how far this can go. If the action succeeds in attaining the goals to which it is directed, and if these goals are justified in the horizons in which they are tested, there will be no incentive to re-examine the choice of horizon which led to the positing of these goals. A male psychoanalyst could work with women throughout his professional career, adjusting his theory to his practice, without coming to see that Freud's fundamental view of the male—female relation is in need of radical change. That view informed theory and practice alike by determining how the situation was perceived, the problem, defined, and the solution, projected. Psychoanalysis is a powerful tool for the unmasking of pretence and the uncovering of assumptions. But, partly because of its success, psychoanalysis has not succeeded in unmasking its own pretences or uncovering its own assumptions. *Radical* self-criticism of the sort needed is an activity distinct from what is usually indicated by the close connection of theory and practice.

Marxists have been perceptive critics of psychoanalysis. They have shown that the hierarchical relation between analyst and patient has blocked the right functioning of the praxis model. But the situation is similar with the Marxist sociology frequently employed by political theologians. It, too, is immensely powerful and illuminating. It defines problems, identifies goals and guides action. This action is often successful, thus tending to confirm the initial sociological theory. Where it is not successful, the theory is revised. But this process does not unmask the relativity of the horizon within which it operates. This failure can be illustrated with the same example; for although Marxists on the whole have been less sexist in their attitudes than have psychoanalysts, they appear only a little less deficient when viewed in the light of contemporary feminist consciousness.[37] Or, again, use of Marxist sociology by Latin American theologians of liberation has done little to free them from implicit anti-Judaism in their theological formulations. Overcoming of sexism or anti-Judaism requires that consciousness be raised through a challenge from a quite different perspective.

I do not intend, however, to pursue the feminist critique, valid and valuable though it is. I use it only to illustrate that the appeal to relevance and praxis cannot assure that our goals will truly be for the indivisible salvation of the whole world. We need to adopt a stance that is more radically self-critical, that is, one which does not predetermine the norms by which self-criticism will take place.

The significance of this example of the limitations of the praxis model is not that it needs supplementation with speculation or abstract thought. Quite the contrary. Feminist insights arose in the practice of women. Women who participated in the struggle for social justice found themselves exploited by the men with whom they shared the struggle. They became aware of an additional dimension of oppression. This insight was sharpened and elaborated in relation to new ways of life and political activities. Development of theory and practice in the feminist movement conforms to the praxis model. The introduction of the feminist perspective in criticism of psychoanalysis and Marxism in no way denies the value and validity of that model.

But the praxis model does not work well in the interaction of diverse communities informed by different experience, different practice, different theory and different horizons of meaning. Each such community, if guided by this model, tends to remain blind to the truth that is realised in the others. As used by Metz the model has been insensitive to feminism and gives little appropriate guidance to efforts to establish new relationships with other religious traditions. We need some understanding of the way truth is realised that goes beyond the ususal formulation of theory and practice. Only so can we guide and illumine the process whereby the truth realised in one community can be appropriated by others as well.

At this point process theology has a contribution to make. Both Wieman and Whitehead saw that truth grows through interchange with those whose experience and understanding are different from ours. The encounter with divergent beliefs challenges our own. The more fundamental the divergence, the greater the challenge and the greater also the opportunity for growth in truth.

Growth in truth cannot be the addition of new, discrepant beliefs to old ones. Nor is it likely to occur if the old beliefs are discarded in favour of the new. Certainly the rejection of the new beliefs cannot help us, and a compromise is little better. Growth occurs when the conflicting beliefs are converted by creative thought into what Whitehead calls a contrast. That is, their distinct integrity and power are retained in their mutual tension. But a new understanding or perspective is attained in which the truth of each can be realised along with the limitation of each. In this relation each is transformed by its new relation to the other, and the total experience and vision is widened and enriched. We attain a new basis for a new praxis.

When the fundamental importance of this mode of growth is appreciated, final allegiance can no longer be given, as by Sölle, to the gospel's 'non-derivable promise and the demand for peace, freedom, and justice for all people'.[38] This may be the highest claim we can now imagine, but we cannot know whether in confrontation with others — with Buddhists, perhaps — we will discover that this claim, too, is relative. That would not mean its rejection, but it would mean its inclusion within a wider and broader movement toward the realisation of truth. Our ultimate loyalty cannot be given to any existing claim or insight. It must be given to the reality by virtue of which this claim or insight can be relativised as we advance in truth. That reality is the ground of the novelty which makes it possible to convert mutually exclusive conflict into contrast.

There are apparent similarities between growth through contrast and the dialectical process of the Hegelian and Marxist traditions. Indeed, in some formulations of the dialectic, the results may be identical. Nevertheless, the usual understanding and application of the dialectic do not lead to the radical openness that is needed, the readiness to encounter the simply unexpected or the tradition that has developed out of quite alien assumptions. In both Hegel and Marx the negation is directed at the affirmation. The contrasting idea, for process thought, may have developed within an entirely different horizon of meaning and interest. At the very least, the idea of contrast needs to challenge the dialectician to deal with a wider range of traditions and modes of thought with greater attention to their autonomous meanings.

NOTES

1   See 'Thematic issue: New Testament interpretation from a process perspective', *Journal of the American Academy of Religion* (March 1979).
2   Dorothee Sölle, *Political Theology*, trans. John Shelley (Philadelphia, Pa.: Fortress Press, 1974), pp. 15—16 and 73.
3   *Ibid.*, p. 24.
4   Shirley Jackson Case, *Evolution of Early Christianity: a Genetic Study of First-Century Christianity in Relation to its Religious Environment* (Chicago, Ill.: University of Chicago Press, 1914), p. 22—3.
5   Sölle, *Political Theology*, p. 76.
6   See James M. Robinson, 'Hermeneutic since Barth' in James M. Robinson and John B. Cobb, Jr., ed., *The New Hermeneutic* (New York: Harper & Row, 1964), pp. 30—3; See also Rudolf Bultmann *et al.*, *Kerygma and Myth: a Theological Debate* (New York: Harper & Bros., 1961), pp 39—40.
7   Sölle, *Political Theology*, p. 65.

8   *Ibid.*, p. 64.
9   Johann Baptist Metz, *Faith in History and Society: Toward a Practical Fundamental Theology*, trans. David Smith (New York: Seabury Press, 1980). p. 201.
10   *Ibid.*
11   *Ibid.*
12   Johann Baptist Metz, *Befreiendes Gedächtnis Jesu Christ* (Mainz: Matthias-Grünewald Verlag, 1970) translation in Roger Dick Johns, *Man in the World: the Political Theology of Johannes Baptist Metz* (Missoula, Mont.: Scholars Press, 1976), p. 109.
13   Metz, *Faith in History and Society*, p. 165.
14   *Ibid.*, p. 166.
15   H. Richard Niebuhr, *The Meaning of Revelation* (New York: MacMillan, 1941).
16   Metz, *Faith in History and Society*, p. 119.
17   *Ibid.*, p. 168.
18   *Ibid.*, p. 196.
19   *Ibid.*, p. 162.
20   *Ibid.*, p. 166.
21   *Ibid.*, p. 165. This point is made repeatedly. See pp. ix and 76.
22   *Ibid.*, p. 50.
23   *Ibid.*, p. 54.
24   *Ibid.*, p. 68.
25   'Toward the critique of Hegel's philosophy of right', in Marx and Engels, *Basic Writings on Politics and Philosophy*, ed. L.S. Feuer (New York: Anchor Books, 1959), p. 245.
26   Ernst Bloch, *On Karl Marx*, trans. John Maxwell (New York: Herder & Herder, 1971), p. 168.
27   Jürgen Moltmann, *Religion, Revolution and the Future*, trans. M. Douglas Meeks (New York: Charles Scribner's Sons, 1969), p. 138.
28   Sölle, *Political Theology*, p. 74.
29   *Ibid.*, p. 75, quoted from Jürgen Habermas, *Theorie und Praxis*, vol. 2 of *Politica* (Berlin: Luchterhand, 1963), p. 316.
30   Sölle, *Politcal Theology*, p. 75.
31   *Ibid.*, p. 76.
32   Dorothee Sölle, *Beyond Mere Dialogue: On Being Christian and Socialist* (Detroit, Mich.: American Christians Toward Socialism, 1978), p. 14.
33   Sölle, *Political Theology*, pp. 75–6.
34   Johann Baptist Metz and Trutz Rendtorff, eds., *Die Theologie in der interdisziplinören Forschung* (Düsseldorf: Bertelsmann Universitatsverlag, 1971).
35   There is, of course, no one praxis model. The variety of ways theologians have conceived the relation of theory and practice are analyzed by Matthew Lamb in 'The theory-praxis relationship in contemporary Christian theologies', *CTSA: Proceedings of the*

Thirty-First Annual Convention, 1976, pp. 149—78. I am understanding by the praxis model loosely what he calls 'critical praxis
correlations'.

36   Alfred North Whitehead, *Adventures of Ideas* (New York: The Macmillan Company, 1933), part I.

37   See Rosemary Ruether, *New Woman/New Earth: Sexist Ideologies
and Human Liberation* (New York: Seabury Press, 1975), pp.
162—85.

38   Sölle, *Political Theology*, p. 76.

Chapter Four

THE DOCTRINES OF GOD
AND ESCHATOLOGY

In the thirties interest at Chicago turned away from the socio-historical school because of two weaknesses. First, it seemed to be bound up with a generally optimistic expectation that human efforts, spearheaded by Christians, would bring into being a better society. The writings of Reinhold Niebuhr destroyed this optimism and turned attention to the question of finding meaning in history without the illusion of stable progress. Second, the socio-historical school failed to offer a satisfactory way of thinking of God. In a situation in which inherited ideas of God had become incredible, it was necessary to reconceive God. Chapter Two briefly surveyed the responses of Wieman, Hartshorne and others to this dual problem.

The negative aspect of this work, as already stressed, was that it in fact separated theology from its socio-political matrix and established it instead in the context of the history of ideas. To work back from that to a new form of political theology has been a slow and arduous task. Yet to those who participated in or benefited from the wrestling with historical meaning and the concept of God, there seems no reason to forget what was learned. Political theology, too, must deal with these questions. During the past fifteen years political theology has too much avoided the conceptual issues that are involved with these doctrines. Process theology has something to contribute.

Section I summarises what Sölle, Moltmann, and Metz understand by God. Section II shows how the thought about God of Wieman and Whitehead can complement the work of the political theologians in needed ways. Section III offers a process eschatology as a solution to certain problems in German political theology.

I

Rudolf Bultmann directed most of his attention to the understanding of human existence and faith. This did not imply any lack of belief in God as one who acted. In his view faith understands itself as the pure gift of God, a God who is imaged as acting from above and may be thought of by analogy with human persons.

This image of God's spatial transcendence was not accepted by Bultmann's more influential students, and in their writings the meaning of the word 'God' became less clear. The focus of attention was more unqualifiedly on the actual situation which was viewed in a more fully historical way. Although most Bultmannians did not go so far, Dorothee Sölle's qualified acceptance of the idea of the 'death of God' did not involve a major break.

Sölle does not stop speaking of God. But she rejects theism without compromise — 'the omnipotent God, the king, father, and ruler, who is above the world'.[1] The God of whom she speaks after the death of this God is a powerless and helpless God:

> In all religions, a question mark has been set against the omnipotent and serene gods by the sufferings of men. But only in Christ does the concept of a suffering God appear. Here alone is it the suffering of God which is shouldered by a man. Only in Christ does it become clear that we can put God to death because he has put himself in our hands. Only since Christ has God become dependent on us. Christ did not identify himself with a calm spectator of all our troubles. Christ, by his teaching, life and death, made plain the helplessness of God in the world; the suffering of unrequited and unsuccessful love.[2]

If one asks for conceptual clarification of Sölle's idea of God, the answer is not clear. She is speaking of how human beings have experienced whatever they have called God. It seems that for her 'God' now means something very much like love, the love which she says is unrequited and unsuccessful and expresses the helplessness of God in the world.

However that may be, God is not for Sölle a power or agent alongside human power or agency with which human beings are to reckon. God is found in human actions or nowhere. Control over those actions is in human hands. If God who 'suffers by reason of his unrealised, or only partly realised, existence in the world'[3] is to be more fully realised, that must be through free human action expressive of love.[4]

In *Political Theology* Sölle draws the implications of this understanding of God explicitly. She rejects apocalyptic hope in favour of prophetic hope, in which the outcome depends upon human obedience.[5] She asks rhetorically: 'Can God — independently of whatever "the world," and therefore society, does or fails to do — bestow forgiveness directly on a penitent man and make possible a new beginning for him?'[6] Her consistent view of political theology is that it declares that the future is in our hands and that we are called by Jesus's message to embody love in the world.

Although Sölle's comments about God are largely negative, this is not because she is opposed to using language about God altogether. What she opposes is language about God that depreciates human responsibility or expresses ideology. She believes that the idea of God as a totally free and independent being expresses the ideals of the entrepreneur and the macho male rather than anything to be found in Jesus.[7] In much of her writing there are few constructive suggestions to oppose to the traditional rhetoric that she finds objectionable.

More recently, however, she has hinted at more positive formulations.

> The more I grew in the socialist movement, the more I discovered a new God-language. The point for me is not merely to overcome a sexist language by changing the pronouns, because a female imagery can include domination and wrong protection as well. I think it is more important to overcome the inherent substantial machismo in the God-talk, its bourgeois male ideals. The adoration of power and independence established the eternal alien determination of human-kind. When one of the main political goals of democratic socialists is the workers' co-determination and self-control, how can we stand a God-talk based on the refusal of democratization and self-determination? If God is not ready to give up his power, if he does not want us to determine our fate, we cannot trust him. He is then nothing but a somewhat liberal capitalist, and our trust in that end would make us more childish than we are. The God we are in need of is not a private owner, nor a capitalist with a human face. There is only one legitimization of power and that is to share it. Power which is not shared, in other words, which is not transformed into love, is domination; to adore it means to will slavery.[8]

Metz and Moltmann also reject the theistic God and see God in the suffering of Jesus. They, too, reject images of God as spatially transcendent or above. Hardly more than Sölle do they encourage thought of God as an agent alongside other agents, one who brings things about in the world or in human life. But it is clearer in their cases than in Sölle's that 'God' is not an expendable word. Metz writes, for example, that 'the name of God stands for the fact that the utopia of the liberation of all human subjects is not a pure projection which is what that utopia would be if it were only a utopia and no God'.[9]

Although Moltmann speaks a great deal about God, he rarely addresses directly the question, Who is God? On one occasion when he does so, he writes as follows:

> What do we mean by the word 'God'? The image of the authority in heaven, which one can accuse, justify, deny or affirm, is past. The judging God is found in the man who argues with God. The glory of the totally other world of God as a transforming power in this world is present in the Christ who was forsaken by God and sacrificed by him. In this way, we abandon the centuries-old, weak Christianization of the God concept and are on the way towards a fuller understanding of God in the crucified Christ. Who is 'God' in the Christ event? He is the power of the transformation of the world in vicarious suffering. Who is 'God' in the corresponding event of belief in unbelief? He is the word of the justification of the godless. Who is 'God' in the event of love and alienation? He is the power of freedom in self-surrender. Who is 'God' in the event of hope in the face of death? He is the power of a qualitatively new future. Finally, who is 'God' in the new creation? He is the eternal presence of the victory of the crucified Christ.[10]

These paradoxical statements could be interpreted to mean much the same as what Sölle affirmed, except that, as in Metz, the note of futurity is much stronger here. 'The God spoken of here is no intra-worldly or extra-worldly God but the "God of hope" (Rom. 15.13), a God with "future as his essential nature" (as E. Bloch puts it), as made known in Exodus and in Israelite prophecy, the God whom we therefore cannot really have in us or over us but always only before us, who encounters us in his promises for the future, and whom we therefore cannot "have" either, but can only await in active hope.'[11]

Moltmann does not speak of God's powerlessness or helplessness in quite the way Sölle does, but no more than for her is God a controlling power or even a distinguishable agent of action in the world. God's power appears in the power of the promise by which we are drawn into the future. That promise which is given in the crucified Christ is the determinant of Christian life.

Sölle too speaks of a promise along with a demand, but she makes clear that the realisation of the promise is a function of obedience to the command. Moltmann, on the other hand, makes use of apocalyptic imagery alongside of the prophetic. Sölle complains that his theology of hope is 'a mythology of apocalyptic promise'.[12] But Moltmann stresses also the openness of the future and the element of risk. It is not clear, at least to this writer, whether Moltmann believes the promise will someday really be fulfilled, whether he thinks it may be fulfilled, or whether his concern is entirely for the meaning of life here and now in light of the promise, so that the question of its actual fulfilment in the future does not arise. Systematically it is difficult to see how one can be confident of a future realisation of the promise when there is no transcendent divine power that can insure victory over the enormous historical threats which we face. But if Moltmann does not intend the promise to give us assurance, his apocalyptic language is misleading.

Unlike Sölle and Moltmann, Metz struggled with the doctrine of God in a philosophical context. But just as Sölle left behind the God of Bultmann, and Moltmann turned away from the God of Barth, so also Metz criticised the God of transcendental Thomism. For him, too, history becomes the encompassing horizon even for our understanding of God. God is found in the self-reflection of human understanding. There God is disclosed in and with human subjectivity. God is the 'subjectivity of the subjectivity of man' which is understood especially as the 'freeing freedom of human freedom'[13] or the 'transcending willedness of the will' which is 'the ground of every particular self-realization' of the will.[14] God is the ground and origin of the will by being the end, the fulfilment toward which it is called. Human beings are not called thereby away from themselves but to their true selves. 'God as the final end is the encompassing whither of human self-realization.'[15]

This idea of the whither of fulfilment led Metz increasingly to agree with Moltmann that the future is God's essential nature. It led him to similar views of the future as promise constituting the horizon for political action in the world. But Metz is more explicit that there is a 'possibility of being defeated',[16] and he wrestles more painfully with the difficulty of apocalyptic hope.[17]

Metz meditates at length on the apocalyptic consciousness in its contrast with the dominant modern one, which he calls evolutionary. By evolutionary he does not mean teleological but rather infinite and so in fact timeless:

> Apocalyptic consciousness ... calls the timeless understanding of time that has become so firmly established in theology into question. This [timeless] understanding of time enables theology to regard itself as a kind of constant reflection that is institutionally protected and cannot be interrupted by any imminent expectation, without pressure of activity or surprises and experienced in rendering harmless expectations that are open to disappointment, but are nonetheless genuine.[18]

Metz wants to restore a consciousness of time within which the apocalyptic hope can live.

It is difficult to see, however, how the apocalyptic expectation can be justified without a type of belief in God which seems alien to Metz. It developed in a world in which God as a powerful agent could act upon the world from without. In that context it made sense. But Metz seems not to affirm such a God any more than Sölle or Moltmann.

II

All three theologians believe that the future is open, replete with truly new possibilities. All believe that human beings are called to realise possibilities of love, to withdraw from present structures of oppression and injustice, and to actualise the possibilities of liberation and justice. All associate God with this open future and its possibilities for good. Both Sölle and Moltmann emphasise God's suffering in and with humanity. With all of this process theologians are in enthusiastic agreement.[19]

But these important gains of the political theologians are won at a high price with respect to the doctrine of God. The idea of God is fairly clear in Bultmann, Barth and Rahner. Process theologians are critical of their doctrines of God and hence welcome the criticisms of the German political theologians. We share in the emphasis on God's suffering and we rejoice in the association of God with what makes human beings free and gives them an open future of unrealised possibilities. But the conceptual formulations by the three German political theologians are so vague that the consequences could be dangerous for the future of Christian faith in God.

The negative consequences are clearest in Sölle. 'God' has virtually ceased to be an operative word with her. What she has to say can be said more clearly without using it. Her clarity is admirable, but the implications are serious. Her political theology is a matter of loyalty to Jesus and strenuous exertion to achieve justice and righteousness in human society. That is commendable. But Christians know something of the limits of such efforts. We know the need of the sense of being borne by a power not ourselves, being directed by a wisdom greater than our own, and being accepted even as we fail. None of this can be affirmed by Sölle. Hers is a Christianity for heroes.

Yet by a little reflection, and without violating her admirable commitments, one could see grace at work in her world. Her great concern is that the institutions of society be transformed, and she calls human beings to take full responsibility for that transformation. But she knows that only transformed people will transform society. 'Political theology prods men to combat their own apathy, creating new anguish and inspiring new projects. It entices them to seek transformation.'[20] In this formulation there seems to be some recognition that we cannot simply transform ourselves by an act of choice. We must seek transformation. Could we say we must allow transformation to occur in us? Such allowing is an activity, a responsible one, but it is different from the attempt to manipulate ourselves.

This difference was at the heart of Wieman's work which was summarised in Chapter Two. He distinguished the created goods from the creative good. Our present commitments and ideals, including those of Sölle, are created goods. They have resulted from a process which worked through our social interactions. But now, once established, they are created goods. If we take them as ultimate and act and organise to preserve and expand them, we will be closed to the needed transformation even of our best commitments and ideals. If we truly seek transformation, we must open ourselves to the creative good that works in and through our interactions with others. Grace thus has the primacy, but not a grace that supersedes or undercuts human activity. It is a grace that operates in our efforts.

The recognition of this creative good is important not only as we seek transformation but as we conceive of those structures of justice and liberation that we wish to build. The absolutisation of our present ideas and ideals leads to efforts to embody them in the new structures. Recognition that the true good is a process of transforming ideas and ideals leads to striving for structures that allow that good to work. Instead of rejecting every idea of an active and acting God when she rejects classical theism, Sölle might profit from approaching empirically the working of grace as Wieman did. Such a grace can be seen also to forgive in the sense of enabling one, anyone, 'to begin anew'.[21] This is, of course, not the forgiveness 'from above' against which Sölle polemicises. It is precisely the gift of new beginnings which takes place in human interactions. But the gift is not from the individuals with whom one interacts. One needs forgiveness from them, too, but that does not replace divine forgiveness. To be sensitive to the creative process, to open oneself to its working, to direct others to it, is no trivial matter.

Metz and Moltmann have not rejected grace in their rejection of the traditional theistic God. God is important to them, and belief in God is effective in their theologies. Nevertheless, what they mean by the word God remains elusive. They provide powerful images, some of which have been noted above. It is by such images that theology most directly shapes the life of the Christian. Further, they form these images in such a way as to direct Christian energies toward the liberation of the oppressed. This is a major achievement, and process theologians have much to learn from it. But, as Ogden notes with respect to liberation theologians, they 'focus on the existential meaning of God for us without dealing at all adequately with the metaphysical being of God in himself'.[22] To reject the conceptual task of theology reflects an inadequate understanding of how faith functions. It is true that we are more immediately affected by images than by concepts and that through Christian history much of the attention of theologians has been properly directed to the fashioning and refashioning of images. But images are powerful only when those who hold them believe, consciously or unconsciously, that the images are appropriate to reality. When images are used to move us without convincing us that they are appropriate to reality, they are felt as manipulative rather than liberating and energising. Propaganda consists in such images. Theology should not. Even when images have a life and power of their own which cannot be exhausted by analysis, theology cannot avoid the conceptual and discursive questions of their meaning and truth.

Where readers are not helped to arrive at a new concept of God, they will continue to hear in the word 'God' what that word has meant in the tradition. These meanings have often been in tension with the thrust of political theology. Devotion to God as typically conceived traditionally has encouraged a quest for inner purity which is not recognised as bound up with the socio-political situation. God's eternity and immutability have been contrasted with the ephemeral character of historical events in such a way as to depreciate efforts at social transformation. God's omnipotence suggests that the course of events is finally in God's hands, not ours, and that our feeble efforts to shape the course of history are misguided. The political theologians reject this concept of God. But when they fail to clarify an alternative concept, they cannot complete their mission. Worship is likely to be directed still to a God who is consciously or unconsciously conceived as eternal, immutable and omnipotent in that sense that introduces a tension between the depths of the worshipper's devotion and the call to participate in historical liberation.

Alternatively, if the readers see that this concept of God is rejected and cannot find a new one to which to relate the powerful images of political theology, they may decide that the meaning of what is said can be clarified without use of this word. Perhaps it can be replaced by 'the hoped-for future'. They will suppose the word is used now chiefly for rhetorical effect, and that translation into the language of atheistic humanism will be a gain. But with that, too, much of the power of political theology will be lost.

What is needed is a new concept of God which will fit with the rich imagery of political theology and ground its existential meaning. This idea of God must be such that, in Metz's words, 'the struggle for God and the struggle to enable all men to be free subjects does not operate in the opposite direction, but proportionally in the same direction'.[23] Process theologians believe they have found the conceptuality that is needed in the philosophy of Alfred North Whitehead. It is for this reason that his ideas about God have struck deep roots through five decades of study. They are not easy ideas to grasp, and in isolation from his whole system of thought they prove less convincing. But a brief exposition may show how they can claim to meet the needs of political theology.

First, consider the totality of reality, including human experience, as a vast field of events. Each event comes into being out of its past. The new event could not be what it is if it did not have exactly the past which it does have, and it cannot be anything which that past does not allow it to be. There is, therefore, a great deal of determination of what happens now by what has happened up until now.

Second, consider the normal approach of the sciences to the understanding of the new event. The scientific task is to explain the event, and the task of explaining it is generally understood to be to show how antecedent circumstances led necessarily to its being what it is. That is, the scientific enterprise seeks to explain why the event has the form it has by describing the world out of which it comes to be. So far as their scientific work is concerned, virtually all natural and social scientists are determinists. To explain something is usually assumed to be to show why it had to be what it was.

Thus almost of necessity science adopts a methodological determinism, and Whitehead believes that when we restrict our vision to this field of events, we have no basis for opposing a metaphysical determinism as well. What the new event becomes must derive from something, and if all that is is the field of past events, then it must derive from that. If it derives exclusively from that, it must be fully determined by that. If we reject this determinism, it can only be in the name of sheer indeterminism or chance.

Yet there is reason to believe that my own experience, as a crucial example, is not simply explicable in terms of chance and determination by the past. I seem to have some responsibility for what I become. And that is possible only if I exercise some determination upon myself. Further, that determination cannot be only the influence of a past decision upon present experience; for then the present experience would still be fully determined from without, and the past decision in its turn would have been a product of determinism and chance. The decision must decide about itself. Or to put it another way, each event or experience must to some degree be self-determining.

Whitehead believes that indeed there is an element of self-determination in every unitary event or, as he prefers to say, in every occasion of experience. But how is this possible? A decision is only possible among relevant alternatives, but it is not in the nature of the past to constitute itself into such alternatives. The past operates on the present with the force of necessity as efficient cause. If there are relevant alternatives, there must be a sphere of possibility which can be distinguished from the sphere of past actuality. An occasion of experience must receive not only the actuality of the past but also alternative possibilities for its own self-constitution. These possibilities must be relevant to the actual situation, but they must transcend it. They may include the possibility of being passively shaped by the past, but they must include also the possibility not to be simply the outcome of the efficient causality of the past. In short, the relevant possibilities include possibilities of relative novelty.

The effective presence of these relevant novel possibilities for self-constitution does not determine just how an occasion of experience will in fact constitute itself. The possibilities function persuasively as 'lures for feeling'. Thereby they create freedom, a freedom which differs from both determinism and chance. In each occasion of experience a space is opened up for the decision of that occasion about itself. Of course much about that occasion *can* be predicted on the basis of the efficient causality of the past. But, in Whitehead's words, although 'whatever is determinable is determined, ... there is always a remainder for the decision'[24] of that occasion. This remainder is far larger in human experience than in most other occasions of experience, but no event is wholly determined without remainder by its past.

Whitehead believes that the cosmic activity through which relevant potentiality becomes effective in each occasion of experience is properly called God. This is, more precisely, the Primordial Nature of God — God as the organ of novelty. No event occurs in the world without God's coming, not as a part of its past, determining world, but as the gift of freedom, the gift of transcendence, the gift of the future.

III

It is a merit of political theologians to have restored eschatology to the heart of Christian theology. Moltmann points out that eschatology has often been an appendage, discussed only after the main points have been made without reference to it.[25] In opposition to this tactic he insists that theology is eschatological through and through. That is, the Christian is fundamentally oriented to God's future, and all Christian teaching is to be formulated in the light of that orientation. *The Theology of Hope* goes far toward showing what that means.

Nevertheless, the foregoing summaries of the views of Sölle, Moltmann and Metz have showed that there are problems with the eschatology. It is hard to determine how seriously we may expect or hope for the promised world. Yet the meaning of the hope for us depends on whether it is a real possibility. Let us consider the alternatives.

Prior to World War I many Christians could associate Christian hope with their sense of the progress of civilisation. The social gospel, including the socio-historical school at Chicago, was tinged by this optimism. In the context of such expectation, action for social justice was encouraged. One could be on the side of history and of God in working for justice for oppressed classes.

But World War I and its aftermath shattered this optimistic spirit. It was much more difficult to anticipate a righteous society as a possibility in history. The danger was that, as a result, Christians would cease to be motivated to work in the public arena. Reinhold Niebuhr dealt with this problem with great honesty but also with pathos. 'In the task of ... redemption,' he wrote,

> the most effective agents will be men who have substituted some new illusions for the abandoned ones. The most important of these illusions is that the collective life of mankind can achieve perfect justice. It is a very valuable illusion for the moment; for justice cannot be approximated if the hope of its perfect realization does not generate a sublime madness in the soul. Nothing but such madness will do battle with the malignant power and 'spiritual wickedness in high places.' The illusion is dangerous because it encourages terrible fanaticisms. It must therefore be brought under the control of reason. One can only hope that reason will not destroy it before its work is done.[26]

One response to the dilemma articulated by Niebuhr is to renew the doctrine that in fact a perfect outcome of the historical process is to be anticipated. This is the strategy of Teilhard de Chardin and Wolfhart Pannenberg. There is little doubt that there is much in the Biblical witness that supports this doctrine and that the expectation of such a final End to history has been foundational to much of Christian theology throughout the centuries. If Christian faith can be renewed as the confident anticipation of a final resurrection of all from the dead, then belief in the future attainment of justice and righteousness is not, after all, an illusion. It is sober fact in the light of which all life is most realistically to be lived.

Process theology shares with Metz, Moltmann and Sölle an unwillingness or inability to participate in this confident anticipation of a consummation of the historical process. Instead, history is really open. But if this openness means, as Niebuhr often seemed to say, that social gains are all ephemeral, that the problems that arise are as serious as the ones that are solved, that indeed work for social righteousness is Sisyphean, then few will give themselves to it.

Niebuhr himself came to recognise that he may have overstated the case when he had asserted that we must believe that perfect justice is possible in order to be optimally motivated.[27] We can be inspired to committed effort by the conviction that a situation much better than the present one is realistically obtainable. The knowledge that the new situation, too, will be flawed will not deter us. On the whole this sufficed in the earlier Social Gospel. Its leaders did not believe that the society they were building was the Kingdom of God, but they did believe that human obedience to God could usher in a world in which many of the present social evils would be overcome. Subsequent events were disillusioning, but one option for a political theology which does not want to commit itself to belief in a real consummatory End is to arouse hopes of relatively unambiguous change for good in society. Among Latin American liberation theologians this is often, even usually, what is hoped for. A socialist revolution is anticipated as bringing an end to the massive oppression of present society without introducing new evils of comparable magnitude. Working for such a revolution is experienced as inherently meaningful. Discussing the new problems that such a revolution will bring is usually regarded as unnecessary and inappropriate. Nevertheless, these theologians are careful to deny that the more just societies for which they hope can be identified with the Kingdom of God. Belief in this Kingdom functions to relativise every human attainment. But how we are to conceive this Kingdom is unclear.

Sölle's view is quite straightforward. It does not focus on the Kingdom of God and its relation to a new society to be brought into being by humanity. For her, faith is freedom from every belief in a fixed order or human nature. She sees liberation as a real possibility in history, and she understands faith as 'trust in the ongoing process of liberation'.[28] This trust entails no assurance of a successful outcome in the course of history. As far as it goes her position is the same as that of process theology, but it does not seem to wrestle with the eschatological question of ultimate meaning.

Metz suggests that there is another possibility. He proposes that all the reflections in which we have been engaged presuppose an understanding of time that is different from the apocalyptic one within which Christianity arose. If we can free ouselves from the dominant sense of endless time and recover the apocalyptic vision, then the New Testament experience of hope can become real for us. Some of his theology seems to presuppose this point of view.

Process theologians cannot follow Metz here. He himself rejects the cosmology of the Bible and even its conceptions of God. It seems arbitrary to argue for a view of time which appears to be bound up with that cosmology and that view of God. We stand, therefore, before a radically open future with no assurance that our efforts for justice will succeed or even that human history will long continue. We too need to ground our political concerns in an eschatological hope. We do not find that this has been done in a convincing way by Sölle, Moltmann or Metz. We turn again to Whitehead for whom also the eschatological question was the central existential or religious one.

For Metz and Moltmann there is a close relationship between what they mean by God and the promise by which they live. For Teilhard and for Pannenberg there is an even more complete identity between God and the eschaton. For Teilhard God is Omega or that final consummation toward which all life on this planet has moved. For Pannenberg God *is* the Kingdom of God or the universal resurrection. For Whitehead also the eschaton is virtually identified with God.

To explain this, we will need to consider an aspect of Whitehead's thought not dealt with above, one to which Hartshorne directed his primary attention. To be at all, for Whitehead, as for Hartshorne, is to feel or, in more technical language, to prehend. An occasion of experience prehends its past world, that is, takes aspects of that past world into its own constitution. For the most part it is the force of the past events that determines what is felt and to what degree; so what is prehension from the side of the new event is causality from the side of the past ones. Also, as soon as this new event of feeling is complete, it becomes part of the past world and compels future occasions to take account of it. It is thus the nature of every occasion of experience to be first a subject constituting itself through the prehension of past events and relevant possibilities and then an object which enters into the constitution of subsequent events.

We have seen that God enters into the constitution of every occasion in the form of relevant possibilities or lures for feeling. Whitehead believed that there is a deep religious intuition that God like all other actualities is also affected by all things. He also showed that there are philosophical reasons supporting this intuition. Thus Whitehead envisioned God's immanence in the world and also the world's immanence in God. The divine inclusion of the world — a different world, of course, in every moment — is the Consequent Nature of God. Like Hartshorne, Whitehead is convinced that apart from some such final, though ongoing, consummation of the world, the ground of meaningfulness of human action and concern is undermined.

Because all that I am and do is taken up into the divine life along with all the consequences of my acts in the lives of others, I cannot escape the seriousness, the importance, of how I use my freedom. I see the truth of the idea that everything I do to my neighbour I do also to God. I can experience God's acceptance of my efforts, even when they fail. Because the Consequent Nature of God takes up into itself all that I am and do and all the consequences of my life, I must also recognise that my failure to respond forever forecloses some possibilities, and that the injuries I inflict on others cannot be undone.

Whitehead was sensitive to an objection that might be raised at this point. What would it really mean for God to include forever all the suffering and sin of human history? Would it mean that even in God there is no redemption? Whitehead's response was to consider how in human experience there can be a kind of redemption of past suffering and sin. The consequences of my past suffering and sin remain in my experience now, but it is possible that they have been so transmuted through my growth and repentance as to enrich rather than degrade my present life. Whitehead envisions that in the divine life, far more than in the human, there is a redemption of the evil of the world, a redemption which does not remove its evil, but which includes it within a whole to which even human evil can make some positive contribution, however limited. God suffers with us, but the suffering does not destroy God as it can destroy us.

The relevance of Whitehead's thought for eschatology needs further exposition. In the first place, his position provides no grounds for doubting the possibility, even the likelihood, that we human beings will destroy ourselves. For this reason it cannot assure us of the meaningfulness of our actions by pointing toward a future Kingdom of God on this planet. On the other hand, Whitehead by no means precludes the possibility of drastic changes for the better taking place in the future. There is no inevitability about our imminent extinction. There is no special likelihood that the patterns of future events will continue those of the recent past. The course of life on this planet has involved many drastic changes, and there is no reason to suppose that it has now arrived at permanent stability.

This is a point at which Whitehead is closer to Teilhard de Chardin than to Niebuhr and Moltmann. The latter view our situation and our expectations in terms of rather short time spans. Niebuhr, for example, takes recent European history as his basic context for projecting the future. Teilhard and Whitehead, in contrast, encourage a view of thousands, even of millions, of years. This longer view displays far more radical changes and indicates the possibility of great advances as well as catastrophes. For example, organised warfare is a matter of the past ten thousand years or less. There is no inherent necessity for it to continue for the duration of history. But, again, there is no assurance that war will not have the last word!

This view that the stakes are very high should not conflict with the emphasis of political theology that we are to be oriented to God's future. However, it does accentuate what is already a problem in much of political theology. If justice and righteousness are not achieved, what then? Are we simply failures? Has God also failed? Is history simply a waste of time and effort?

For Whitehead the ultimate ground of assurance of the worthwhileness of our efforts cannot lie in a future event on this planet.

Such a consummating event, if all goes well, could have penultimate significance, but it would not bring an end to the process. Eventually this planet will become uninhabitable. Our resurrection cannot be here or on any other planet revolving around some other sun. It must be in God.

What is resurrected in God is what has occurred here in the course of natural and historical events. Here is where decisions are made and the content of the Kingdom is detemined. There can be no depreciation of the importance of the historical future in this view. Rather the importance of the historical future and of how we freely shape it is confirmed and undergirded by the truly eschatological resurrection of all things within the divine life. It is important that we should succeed in realising new levels of justice, but even if we fail, our efforts count forever in God.

NOTES

1 Dorothee Sölle, *Christ the Representative: an Essay in Theology After The 'Death of God'*, trans. David Lewis (Philadelphia, Pa.: Fortress Press, 1967), p. 150.

2 *Ibid.*, p. 151.

3 *Ibid.*, p. 149.

4 This note is continued in Dorothee Sölle, *Beyond Mere Obedience*, trans. Lawrence W. Denef (Minneapolis, Minn.: Augsburg Publishing House, 1970), where Sölle can speak positively of God only when God's will is identified with what is 'determined in the situation' (p. 38).

5 Dorothee Sölle, *Political Theology*, trans. John Shelley (Philadelphia, Pa.: Fortress Press, 1971), p. 51.

6 *Ibid.*, p. 100.

7 Dorothee Sölle, 'Remembering Christ', *Christianity and Crisis* (7 June 1976), p. 137.

8 Dorothee Sölle, *Beyond Mere Dialogue: On Being Christian and Socialist*, (Detroit, Mich.: American Christians Toward Socialism, 1978), p. 38. For a congenial discussion of power from the process perspective see Bernard M. Loomer, 'Two conceptions of power', *Process Studies* (spring, 1976), pp. 5–32.

9 Johann Baptist Metz, *Faith in History and Society: Toward a Practical Fundamental Theology*, trans. David Smith (New York: Seabury Press, 1980), p. 67.

10 Jürgen Moltmann, *Hope and Planning*, trans. Margaret Clarkson (New York: Harper & Row, 1967), p. 16.

11 Jürgen Moltmann, *Theology of Hope*, trans. James W. Leitch (New York: Harper & Row, 1967), p. 16.

12   Sölle, *Political Theology*, p. 51.
13   Johann Baptist Metz, *Christliche Anthropozentrik: Über die Denk-form des Thomas von Aquin* (Munich: Kosel Verlag, 1962), p. 76. (My translation.)
14   *Ibid.*, p. 75. (My translation.)
15   *Ibid.*, p. 78. (My translation.)
16   Metz, *Faith in History and Society*, p. 162.
17   *Ibid.*, p. 169–79.
18   *Ibid.*, p. 177.
19   Sölle and Moltmann have both recognised points of contact with process theology. In dealing with the relation of human to divine activity Sölle has written: 'At this point process theology is very helpful in understanding the concept of liberation.' Dorothee Sölle, 'Resistance: toward a First World theology', *Christianity and Crisis* (23 July 1979), p. 179. Moltmann has quoted Whitehead with approval in his rejection of traditional theism. Jürgen Moltmann, *The Crucified God*, trans. R.A. Wilson and John Bowden (New York: Harper & Row, 1974), p. 250.
20   Sölle, *Political Theology*, p. 69.
21   *Ibid.*, p. 98. It also can be understood as the process of liberation which she encourages us to trust. Dorothee Sölle, 'Remembering Christ', *Christianity and Crisis* (7 June 1976), p. 136.
22   Schubert Ogden, *Faith and Freedom: Toward a Theology of Liberation* (Nashville, Tenn.: Abingdon Press, 1979), p. 34.
23   Metz, *Faith in History and Society*, p. 62.
24   Alfred North Whitehead, *Process and Reality*, corrected ed. by David Ray Griffin and Donald W. Sherburne (New York: The Free Press, 1978), pp. 27–8.
25   Moltmann, *Theology of Hope*, p. 15.
26   Reinhold Niebuhr, *Moral Man and Immoral Society* (New York: Charles Schribner's Sons, 1960), pp. 276–7.
27   Ronald Stone, *Reinhold Niebuhr, Prophet to Politicians* (Nashville, Tenn.: Abingdon Press, 1972), p. 80.
28   Sölle, 'Remembering Christ', p. 156.

Chapter Five

THE POLITICS
OF POLITICAL THEOLOGY

Political theology is political *theology*. It is not theology subordinated to politics. It is the attempt to think faithfully in our time and
situation. But political theology calls on the church to think *politically*. This entails understanding itself and its thought in the concrete socio-historical situation perceived on a global scale.

Many liberation theologians, agreeing to this point with political
theologians, conclude that the church must take sides in political
struggles. This involves, for them, siding with some political programmes and parties against others. It requires the acceptance of
certain political theories and the rejection of others. Specifically,
for many of them, it demands rejection of capitalism and commitment to socialism.

In the light of this call for commitment, the reticence of the
German political theologians, who share so much with liberation
theologians, is striking. They insist that political theology is not a
call to organise or support a particular political programme. The
church should not try once again to impose its will on society. Its
task is first to criticise itself politically and from that perspective
to criticise other institutions as well. In this process it can clarify
the Christian principles in terms of which such criticism takes
place.

Both alternatives are unsatisfactory from the process perspective
expressed in this book. Although many of the goals of socialism
can indeed be affirmed by Christians, there are aspects of socialist
theory and practice of which Christians in general, and process
theologians in particular, have reason to be critical. The assumption,

sometimes tacitly made, that socialism is *the* alternative to capitalism, should be re-examined through a critique of both. Such a criticism will go farther than the German theologians toward development of particular Christian proposals for political theory and practice.

Hence, at this point the book moves from the method and doctrine of theology to reflection on the relevance of Christian teaching for the structure of the political order. The major task of this chapter, dealt with in Section II, is to identify five anthropological themes of political theology that are widely accepted by Christians and to develop their political implications further than the Germans have done. The development will of course reflect the process perspective. Chapters Six and Seven will go beyond this in indicating how a process political theology must oppose the form taken by political theology among the Germans, or at least in Metz. But the account in this chapter is intended only as development of shared convictions, not as opposition.

Before the rudiments of a Christian political theory from the process perspective are presented in Section II, Section I surveys briefly the support for socialism among Christians and the positions taken by the three German political theologians on the relation of theology to politics. This should help to clarify the extent to which the application of shared convictions to political theory and practice is a development of their political theology and the extent to which through this development it offers an alternative view of how theology and political theory and practice are best related.

I

Since the Constantinian establishment the institutional church has generally been allied with the political authorities at least in those countries in which Christianity has been accepted. In modern times this has often meant the alliance of the Christian church with the bourgeoisie and its support of capitalism. Nevertheless, there has also been a Christian current of protest against the dominant class for the sake of the oppressed. In the past hundred years this has frequently expressed itself in support for socialism.

Support for socialism among Christians can be found in the

Social Gospel movement in the United States and parallel movements in Great Britain and on the continent of Europe. These movements were criticised in the further development of theology for their naive identification of Christianity with a social programme and their failure to recognize the limits set by sin to any human accomplishment. But this did not mean that Christian critics of the identification of Christianity with socialism turned against socialism.

Karl Barth, as the greatest theologian of our century, is a particularly important case study. In an address on 'War, socialism, and "Christianity"' in 1915 he stated: 'A true Christian must be a socialist (if he is serious about the reformation of Christianity). A true socialist must be a Christian (if he is concerned with the reformation of socialism).'[1] During the years that followed Barth shifted his position away from this close identification of Christianity and socialism, insisting on the transcendence by Christ of every social form.[2] But Barth remained a committed socialist throughout his life.

In 1919, another of the theological giants of our century, Paul Tillich, called on Christians 'to enter into the socialist movement in order to pave the way for a future union of Christianity and the socialist social order'.[3] Tillich identified himself as a Christian with socialism until he was forced to emigrate by the Nazis. During the early years he was a leader of the 'religious socialist' movement. As he came to see the danger of confusion resulting from this terminology, he spoke instead of a believing realism as the Christian ground of socialism. His socialist writings culminated in *The Socialist Decision* published in 1933 in the shadow of the rising power of the Nazis. In the conclusion he wrote: 'The salvation of European society from a return to barbarism lies in the hands of socialism.'[4] Although Tillich did not emphasise the political side of his thought so strongly during his years in the United States, he did not repudiate it.

The socialist connection was stressed again in the years immediately after World War II. In 1946 Adolf Grimme stated: 'Socialists can be Christians; Christians must be socialists.'[5] This statement was widely accepted among Christians at that time, but when Gollwitzer raised the issue in 1971, the response was highly critical. Wolfhart Pannenberg has pointed out that the ideals which attract Christians to socialism go back to Stoic and Christian sources and are shared by liberalism. 'If the idea of overcoming the lordship of human beings over human beings belongs to the Christian hope ... then it is by no means thereby said that Christians must be socialists in the proper sense. The difference between liberal and socialist ideas appears with respect to the way to attain such a condition.'[6] A Christian decision must be based on careful analysis of actual historical facts, and it is not clear that a Christian can approve either socialism or liberalism without severe reservations. Indeed, Pannenberg argues that the question today is not so much whether a Christian must be a socialist but whether, after observing the actual effects of socialism in Eastern Europe, a Christian can 'still be a socialist in good conscience',[7] that is, a socialist in the strict Marxist sense.

The experience with Marxist socialism in Latin America has been much more positive. The Cuban revolution impresses many Latin American Christians much more by its achievements in liberating the masses from economic oppression than by its suppression of political dissent of discouragement of Christianity. The Allende regime and the Nicaraguan revolution show possibilities for co-operation between Christians and Marxist socialists that go further towards suggesting that socialist revolution can be positively affirmed by Christians. Hence the most serious discussion of the relation of Christianity to socialism has taken place not in Europe but in Latin America.

Many leaders of the Latin church realised in the sixties that the church failed to express its true nature when it continued the age-old alliance with the ruling elite in its oppression of the peasants and workers. The Catholic bishops meeting at Medellin in 1968 firmly declared that the church must express its solidarity with the aspirations of the people of Latin America. They thus sanctioned the liberation theology which has been Latin America's greatest theological gift to the world.

When the Marxist, Salvador Allende, was elected president of Chile in 1970, many Catholic priests supported his programme. A group of eighty issued a call for an international conference that was held in Santiago in 1972.[8] This meeting resulted in the organisation of Christians for Socialism. Although the military coup in 1973 that overthrew and killed Allende changed the situation in Chile radically, Christians for Socialism continued to be an influential force in Latin America and to a lesser extent in North America as well. It held a conference in Toronto in 1974. In 1975, under the leadership of the Maryknoll fathers, a larger conference was held in Detroit, together with Black and feminist theologians, on the Theology of the Americas. This conference recommended study of the socialist option, and five years later at the second Theology of the Americas Conference, this option was approved.

Despite these very significant expressions of Christian support for socialism, the majority position among both Catholics and Protestants in the twentieth century has been against too close an association of Christianity with any political programme or party. Both remember times when the church has sanctioned particular governments and policies, and both are reluctant to move in that direction again. On the other hand, neither desires to separate Christianity from political activity. There are many unresolved issues in this area.

The Catholic hierarchy at times has been supportive of lay involvement in socialist movements, but it has opposed the public commitment of priests to any particular political party or programme. With rare exceptions, such as Sergio Mendez Arceo of Cuernavaca, even bishops who are strongly supportive of liberation theology and practice have stood firmly by this official position. In the United States they have forced priests out of political office. But this does not inhibit the hierarchy from pronouncements on political issues. For example, the American bishops declared in November 1971 that the United States' military action in Vietnam was unjust, and they gave support to selective conscientious objection.

In Protestant circles the issue does not focus so sharply on the activity of ministers. But the conviction that denominations as such should not support particular political parties is equally widespread. Even when the political views of a party run consistently counter to the church's social teachings, the denominations have avoided statements against the party. (Near exceptions can be found. For example, the Presbytery of New York City formally called attention to the opposition between the views of Senator Barry Goldwater and the official teaching of the General Assembly of the United Presbyterian Church when Goldwater ran for president on the Republican ticket.) But they have launched forceful campaigns on such issues as civil rights. And today a conservative segment of Protestantism is organising effectively to implement its nationalistic and anti-socialist ideology.

With respect to the capitalist/socialist issue, both Catholic and Protestant churches have at times made strong statements critical of the former. During the great depression, for example, the 1934 General Assembly of the Presbyterian Church (U.S.A.) urged 'that competition as the major controlling of our economic life be re-examined, and an attempt be made to secure rational planning in our economic life'. It went on to urge further 'that our natural resources and economic institutions be considered as existing for the public good and such plans for ownership and control be delivered as will lead to the best use in the interests of all'.[9] Such statements provide at least implicit support for socialism. But normal, official practice avoids outright endorsement of a political programme. Catholics and Protestants generally agree that Christianity should not allow itself to be identified with any political theory or party.

The German political theologians are sensitive to the charge that political theology aims to renew a tradition in which the church attempts to dictate political theory and policy to society. As a result they are very careful to avoid the appearance of associating Christianity closely with political movement. Although they take a strong stand in solidarity with the oppressed against the oppressors, they generally avoid, at least in their theological writings, committing themselves to any political theory.

Of the three, Metz is the most cautious in this regard. He writes that political theology can assert 'its essentially universal categories "only" as a negative critique in this society. Being a particular element in society, Christianity can only formulate the decisiveness ("absoluteness") and universality of its message without falling into an ideology when it formulates it as critical negation (of and in given situations)'.[10] But this does not, for Metz, exclude positive formulations: 'I understand political theology, first of all, to be a critical correction of present-day theology, inasmuch as this theology shows an extreme privatizing tendency (a tendency, that is, to center upon the private person rather than "public", "political" society). At the same time, I understand this political theology to be a positive attempt to formulate the eschatological message under the conditions of our present society.'[11] Hence, the negative function of political theology in relation to existing social structures has positive import as well. 'Its critical contestation of socio-political conditions is a "determinate negation". It flares up in criticism of very definite conditions. Being a critical attitude to society, it may well take the form, under certain conditions, of revolutionary protest.'[12] Although 'in the pluralistic society it cannot be the socio-critical attitude of the church to proclaim one positive societal order as an absolute norm',[13] nevertheless, the church should have 'the courage to formulate hypotheses suitable to contingent situations'.[14]

In more recent writings Metz continues to be careful not to identify Christian theology with commitment to any particular political theory. However, it is clear that he finds areas of agreement with socialism. Together with Jean-Pierre Jossua he has edited a volume of *Concilium* on *Christianity and Socialism*. In their joint Editorial they say that political theology

> does not make the Kingdom of God the goal of politics and economy. But it insists that the Kingdom of God should not be indifferent to the cost of world markets. It does not confuse God with a utopia to which no one prays. But it insists that religion can earn no greater guilt than from showing its political innocence through non-participation. If the Christian religion is political because it proclaims the dignity of the individual, of the subjective existence of all men and women before God, then it has to stand up for that individuality where it is most endangered. It must not only fight to ensure that people remain individuals, but so that they can grow out of their situation of poverty and oppression to become individuals. That is part of the cost of orthodoxy.[15]

In *Political Theology* Sölle similarly hopes to make clear that here is 'not an attempt to develop a concrete political program from faith'.[16] But political interpretation of the gospel does have a positive as well as a critical meaning. She writes: 'The statement "you are called to freedom" becomes true for wage earners not when they hear it proclaimed, but when it becomes a concrete social actuality: you are called to be self-determining, to cooperate, to organize your own work.'[17]

The gospel's call to workers 'to be self-determining, to cooperate, to organize your own work' clearly implies that it favours some forms of socio-economic organisation over others. Sölle does not consider it appropriate for theology to spell out just what this desirable organisation would be. But she does assert that political theology functions 'both critically and constructively, engaging in ideological criticism and projecting innovative models'.[18]

Subsequent to publication of *Political Theology* Sölle joined the socialist movement and came to identify herself fully as both Christian and socialist. She is renewing the conviction that to be a Christian requires one to be a socialist as well. Of course this does not mean an unqualified approval of all that is done in the name of socialism. Far from it. But it does mean the acceptance of the programme of democratic socialism for overthrowing the power of capitalism.[19]

Moltmann also wishes to keep the distinction between theology and politics clear, but he does provide powerful images of the society for which we are to work and direction for our present practice. After describing the vicious circles of poverty, of force, of racial and cultural alienation, of the industrial pollution of nature and of senselessness and godforsakenness, he proceeds to state what liberation from these involves.

In the *economic dimension of life*, liberation means the satisfaction of the material needs of men for health, nourishment, clothing and somewhere to live. A further part of this is a social justice which can give all members of society a satisfying and just share in the products they produce. In so far as the vicious circle of poverty is produced by exploitation and class domination, social justice can only be achieved by a redistribution of economic power ... If and in so far as socialism ... means the satisfaction of material need and social justice in a material democracy, *socialism is the symbol for the liberation of men from the vicious circle of poverty.*

In the *political dimension of life*, liberation from the vicious circle of oppression also means democracy. By this we mean human dignity in the acceptance of political responsibility. This includes participation in and control of the exercise of economic and political power ... If and to the degree that the democratic movement means the abolition of privilege and the establishment of political human rights, *democracy is the symbol for the liberation of men from the vicious circle of force.*

In the *cultural dimension of life*, liberation from the vicious circle of alienation means identity in the recognition of others. By this we mean the 'human emancipation of man' (Marx), in which men gain self-respect and self-confidence in the recognition of others and fellowship with them. ... If and in so far as emancipation means personalization in socialization and finding one's identity in the recognition of others, *emancipation is the symbol for liberation from the vicious circle of alienation.*

In the *relationship of society to nature*, liberation from the vicious circle of the industrial pollution of nature means peace with nature. No liberation of men from economic distress, political oppression and human alienation will succeed which does not free nature from inhuman exploitation and which does not satisfy nature ... Therefore the long phase of the liberation of man from nature in his 'struggle for existence' must be replaced by a phase of the liberation of nature from inhumanity for the sake of 'peace in existence'. To the degree that the transition from an orientation on increase in the quantity of life to an appreciation of the quality of life, and thus from the possession of nature to the joy of existing in it can overcome the ecological crisis, *peace with nature is the symbol of the liberation of man from this vicious circle.*

In the relationship of man, society and nature to the *meaning of life*, liberation means a significant life filled with the sense of the whole. ... In the background of personal and public awareness, perplexity, resignation and despair are widespread. This inner poisoning of life ... cannot ... be overcome simply by victory over economic need, political oppression, cultural alienation and the ecological crisis ... The absence of meaning and the corresponding consequences of an ossified and absurd life are described in theological terms as godforsakenness ... Faith becomes hope for significant fulfilment. Therefore in the situation of a 'disheartened society', Christian faith becomes 'counting on hope' and is demonstrated through freedom from panic and apathy, from escape and the death-wish. It then leads to courage to do what is necessary, resolutely and patiently, in the vicious circles mentioned above.[20]

This is a beautiful summary of guiding images for practice for which a process theologian can only be grateful. What follows in this chapter and in the succeeding one is in full harmony with what is here expressed. But of course there is more to be considered. Commitment to these symbols must be related more concretely to political theory and practice. The 'innovative models' for which Sölle calls may serve as a middle ground between these symbols and the 'hypotheses suitable to contingent situations' which Metz sees are needed.

Moltmann's care not to identify Christianity with any one political programme or party gave to Latin American theologians of liberation the impression that he, like other European theologians, preferred to remain politically neutral and to theorize only on the universal plane.'[21] Stung by this criticism Moltmann responded in an open letter to Miguez Bonino. He argued that the gospel calls for concrete strategies growing out of real identification with the people at a particular place and time.[22] In Western Europe this means affirming the freedoms already won and then extending 'these democratic rights and freedoms over to economic conditions'.[23] This is the programme of democratic socialism. In Latin America it may sometimes mean 'seeking to overcome class rule and dictatorship of the right by a temporary leftist dictatorship'.[24] But he warns that there are thus far no examples of the democratisation of such a socialism. He concluded characteristically with sharp criticism of specific sins of Christian anti-Marxists in Chile and the Marxist government of Yugoslavia.

This approach of balanced criticism of both liberal capitalism and state socialism in their actual manifestations and practices may well inhibit decisive Christian action in some parts of Latin America, as Moltmann's critics imply. But in the North Atlantic situation it seems appropriate. It would seem appropriate also for Christian theologians to examine the theories underlying practice in both free market and socialist states. Reinhold Niebuhr engaged in such criticism from the perspective of the Christian understanding of history and of human existence. Thus far political theology has contributed little to this important task.[25]

To criticise not only the practice and institutions of both capitalism and socialism but also their theory requires some clarity about the innovative models which Christians should propose. These in turn should reflect what Christians truly believe about human existence and society. The remainder of this chapter is devoted to reflections from the point of view of process thought about five aspects of Christian belief that have relevance to the formulation of innovative models and to the critical evaluation of currently prevalent theories.

II

(1) Christians are committed to the worth of individual persons. This worth is not located in possessions or outward accomplishments. It cannot be measured by the strength or beauty of the body. It does not consist in the usefulness of the individual person to society. It is located in the soul, not as a special substance which merely inhabits a body, but as the locus of the distinctively personal experience of the whole psychosomatic organism. Metz sees that this requires of the church that it should always defend the individual 'from being considered exclusively as matter and means for the building of a completely rationalized technological future'.[26]

Whitehead agrees with and supports these typically Christian views. For him intrinsic value is located in experience. To be an occasion of experience is to have value. The human soul is the flow of personal human experience, and so far as we know it is the locus of supreme value on this planet. Entities other than present experience, including institutions, possessions, laws, customs and even past experiences, have their use as they contribute to the richness of present experience. They are of instrumental value only.

The implication of this for political and economic theory is to some extent obvious and has been assimilated in theories that have arisen within Christendom. Both liberal capitalism and Marxist socialism are committed ultimately to the improvement of the quality of individual experience. Nevertheless, in actual practice both are largely governed by their economic expressions and these involve both theory and practice that are in marked tension with the Christian understanding.

Both capitalism and socialism aim to produce goods in order to satisfy the wants of people as consumers. This aim is laudable from the Christian perspective. But both exaggerate the extent to which consumption of goods can be correlated with richness of experience. In the planned society, further, the question of what goods are to be produced and consumed is decided not by the one whose experience is to be enriched but by some centralised authority. In the capitalist system the consumer has more freedom of choice and thus more control over what is produced. But society, instead of assisting persons to make wise choices, devotes vast sums of money of manipulating choices through advertising.

Both systems may be inherently capable of improvement in these respects. A planned economy can devise methods of making its planning more sensitive to people's preferences, and a free enterprise system can devote attention to consumer education and impose some restrictions on advertising. Nevertheless, there are tendencies in both systems which must be criticised and checked in the light of their own intentions.

More severe criticism is required of the treatment of the human being as producer. Whereas the consumer is in some sense the end of both systems, the producer is viewed primarily as a means. Efficiency is the dominant consideration, and efficiency is judged by the production of goods and services rather than by the increase of enjoyment of work on the part of the labourer. At the theoretical level this is seen most clearly on the capitalist side.

The example of what Louis Brandeis enthusiastically supported as 'scientific management' will clarify this point. Frederick W. Taylor developed this approach for the profoundly humanitarian purpose of enabling workers to achieve their tasks in the most efficient way possible. According to Peter Drucker: 'On Taylor's "scientific management" rests, above all, the tremendous surge of affluence which has lifted the working masses in the developed countries well above any level recorded before, even for the well-to-do.'[27] But this was achieved at a high price. Taylor analysed the work to be done 'into its simplest elements'.[28] He could then assign these simplest performances to the workers. They were not expected to understand the role that these performances played in the whole, and as few decisions as possible were left to them. In Taylor's approach 'the key principle of scientific management ... is separation of thought from action, of conception from performance. The management becomes the mind and the workers the body'.[29]

Marxists have criticised capitalism for this dehumanisation of workers. Workers should not be alienated from their fellow workers and from the fruits of their labour. But this concern for the welfare of the workers is generally subordinated to the concern for efficiency of production in Communist countries as well. Indeed a major attraction of Marxism to underdeveloped countries is the greater ruthlessness it characteristically applies to the goals of building the future society of plenty. Robert Heilbroner describes this superiority of Marxism succinctly:

> There is no secret about the communist blueprint for development. It advocates doing only what every underdeveloped nation must do: reorganizing agriculture to achieve a surplus of food; transferring this surplus to workers who have been released from agriculture; relentlessly, continuously, single-mindedly using these workers to create capital. The difference is that communism, at least in theory, allows the job to be done with much less of the inertia, and friction which hamper it in a non-communist society. Where land is needed, it is taken; where workers are needed, they are moved; where opposition occurs, it is liquidated; where dissent arises, it is suppressed.[30]

Heilbroner's account witnesses to an assumption that development is primarily to be understood as industrialisation. When he wrote, in 1963, this assumption was shared by almost all participants in development policy-making in both capitalist and communist circles. It was bound up with the exaggerated correlation of per capita income and the goal of human development against which the Christian doctrine of the soul should protect us. This assumption is still dominant, but the practical distortions it has introduced into the actual course of 'development' have finally become so apparent that an alternative measure of the success of policies has been proposed by the Overseas Development Council. This is called the Physical Quality of Life Index, and it measures infant mortality, life expectancy, and literacy rather than per capita income. Although these are still very crude indicators of the quality of personal experience, they come one step closer.

Some nations that rejected the dominant style of development measure quite high on this index, whereas others which followed the conventional development path with some success, receive low marks. For example, according to figures published by the Overseas Development Council in 1977 Sri Lanka, which had a per capita annual income of only $130, measured 83 on the Physical Quality of Life Index, whereas Iran, whose per capita annual income was nearly ten times as high, measured only 38.[31] Subsequent events in Iran suggest that the high level of income did not represent much personal satisfaction on the part of masses of people!

There is no more necessity for a free-enterprise or socialist system to dehumanise workers than for it to abuse the freedom of consumers. Even for the sake of the efficiency of production to which both are committed we are learning that worker morale is important and that worker morale can often be improved by more responsible participation by workers in the larger operations of which they are a part.[32] But more than this is needed. The economic theory should be reformulated so as to consider the contribution of the economic process to the richness of experience of the producer on a par with the contribution to the richness of experience of the consumer. That would force a deeper recognition that, in our capacities as consumers as well, there is far less correlation than has been supposed between the richness of human experience and the quantity and quality of goods and services consumed.

(2) Although the first point above accentuates the individualist tendency in Christianity, Christian teaching falls heavily on the side of human solidarity. It has been the merit of the social gospel and of political theology to emphasise this point in the twentieth century,

but it is certainly not new. It was dominant in the Old Testament. In the New Testament Paul and John may be viewed as accentuating the individualist element, but in his image of the church Paul speaks of us as members one of another, and John's gospel employs the imagery of the vine and its branches. We are individuals, but we are individuals who participate in one another and cannot be saved in isolation. Metz picks up this note in Christian teaching, devoting to solidarity the concluding chapter of his major work, *Faith in History and Society*. Indeed 'he views man's *a priori* constitution in terms of shared being in a shared world'.[33]

Much of our Western conceptuality has made it difficult to understand this solidarity of mutual involvement of human beings. The individual mind or the individual organism is often conceived ontologically as self-contained and as related to other individuals only externally. That is, the relation is viewed as incidental to the being of the individual. The individual exists as what he or she is and then, without any essential change, relates to other individuals.

This individualist ontology has been challenged in some forms of idealism, including the Hegelian form which influenced Marx. In this way of thinking, Mind as a whole or, better, *Geist*, is the fundamental reality. Individuals exist through participation in this totality. It is humanity as a whole, that is, *Geist*, which is the fundamental subject of historical development. Or, since individuals differ in their degree of participation in *Geist*, the true history of *Geist* can be traced through those in whom it has manifested itself most fully. In the Marxist transformation the proletariat, in so far as it is conscious of its mission, constitutes the true subject of history.

Neither the individualist ontology nor the collectivist one expresses the Biblical sense of the solidarity of individuals who participate in one another. Whitehead's conceptuality is more helpful. For Whitehead the ultimate individual is a moment of experience. Such an individual does not first exist and then enter into relations with others. On the contrary, it is constituted by its relations and has no other existence than as a creative synthesis of these relations. The richness of its experience is the richness of its relations. The idea of an individual apart from community is nonsensical. Even if we extend the term individual to its usual designation of personal existence from birth to death, the idea of an individual apart from community is meaningless. Persons are communal beings. Rich experience is possible only in community with others whose experiences are rich.

Unfortunately, most economic theory is based on individualist and collectivist views of human beings. The collectivist view encourages the ruthlessness of which Heilbroner wrote. Liberal society is somewhat restrained by its commitment to individuals, but it has paid a high price for its individualist economic theories.

We all know at a common-sense level that we human beings exist in families and communities whose welfare matters greatly to us. A person who is insensitive to the interests of other members of the community or of the community as a whole and seeks only to obtain private wealth is a monster. Yet it is something very much like this monster who is taken as the model of *homo economicus.* Economic activity is viewed as the competition of such persons for scarce resources. Of course, as economists know, *homo economicus* is an abstraction, but we cannot think of human beings in general without abstraction. Further, it has been a highly successful abstraction, illuminating much of our human behaviour. Nevertheless, it is an abstraction from which theory and practice alike have suffered greatly.

It would be idle to question that competition is a fact of life, but it is damaging to elevate it into *the* fact of life. The implication of such an elevation is that the gains of one person are inherently at the expense of others. This is qualified by the confidence of most theorists that as we all behave rationally, that is, seek competitive advantage, the total pool of goods and services will so increase that all will improve their condition. But this does not erase the fact that the theory describes and encourages the quest for competitive advantage.

If instead we view the economic situation from the perspective of relational thinking, we will focus on different examples and derive different principles. Consider a professor who is a member of a faculty. He or she may gain some satisfaction from success in competition with other members of the faculty, for example, from gaining a larger salary at the expense of others. But this cannot go very far. The satisfactions of the professor will depend more on the general quality of life in the institution than on a competitive superiority in income. The quality of the students, the intellectual stimulus from colleagues, the general morale of the community are more important factors in the richness of the professor's experience than the competitive advantage over colleagues. Thus it is more rational for the professor to seek to contribute to the general health of the community than to seek a competitive advantage within it.

The point here is simply that since the richness of our individual experience depends upon the richness of the experience of others with whom we associate, the growth of our good is a function not primarily of competitive advantage but of communal well-being. I have not focused on the economic advantages of the communal approach, but these are not lacking. The same sum of money can accomplish more if its use is planned with a shared sense of the diverse needs of the community. Further, the institution as a whole is likely to increase its resources more if a communal spirit prevails.

This trivial illustration can be magnified by reference to a comparison between German and British industry in the years since World War II. In Germany a more communal spirit prevailed between capital and labour and both have profited. In Britain the mood has been competitive and confrontational, and the British economy has suffered. A realistic economy theory needs to take account of our normal sense of being parts of a larger whole whose welfare is important rather than treating us as self-enclosed individuals whose relations to others are primarily competitive.

The healthy future of the world depends upon a still further extension of the sense of community. We have begun to speak of a world community, and there is an emerging sense of co-humanity with all people. The teachings of most of the world's great religious traditions encourage this recognition of the interconnectedness of all people. One motivation for the limited aid that is now made available by the industrialised nations to the poorer ones is this sense of a global community.

Economists may well say that any such sense of community is too weak to enter into their picture of how individuals and nations operate. But they need to recognise that the model they use works against the strengthening of this community. Since every model helps to shape the events it intends to describe and predict, it is important for the economic model to encourage the growth of the sense of world community. Our existing experiences, and even more our destinies, are bound together. A model of human reality that cannot express this fundamental fact is too abstract and too distorting to be acceptable as a guide to economic behaviour.

The model of competition has dangerous effects in other ways as well. It is expressed in the important role played by the idea of the trade-off. The assumption is that if individually or collectively we satisfy one desire, this will typically be at the expense of satisfying another. It is often argued, for example, that if we satisfy our desire for a clean and healthful environment, we must pay a price in terms of fewer goods and more unemployment.

No one supposes that such a competitive relationship exists between all the goods we desire. Arthur Okun, for example, notes that an increase in equality of opportunity for all can contribute to an increase in efficiency of the economic system. There is no trade-off there. But the basic economic model encourages us to think of trade-off relations as primary and normal. Okun makes his point about equality of opportunity and efficiency in a book entitled *Equality and Efficiency: the Big Tradeoff.*[34] In general, he insists, approximation of equality can only be obtained at the expense of decrease in efficiency.

If we shift to a relational/communal model we cannot do away with all of the oppositions which lead to trade-off thinking. It *is* often the case that we must sacrifice some goods for the sake of others. But we will look primarily for ways in which both desirable variables can be increased in mutually supportive fashion rather than quickly settling for the trade-off. For example, we will challenge the easy assumption that the goals urged by environmentalists can only be attained at the expense of shortage of goods and unemployment. Amory Lovins has argued in detail that an environmentally desirable energy policy will also employ more persons in more desirable ways and produce as much usable power as we need.[35] If we redefine the goal of efficiency as the enhancement of human experience, we are likely to find that most of the oppositions identified by Okun between equality and efficiency will disappear. It may also turn out that more policies can be devised to increase equality in ways that even increase the production of material goods.

(3) The Christian tradition with considerable consistency has affirmed that human actions are not controlled by fate and are not the mere outcome of natural necessity. We are responsible for what we do. We are under bondage to many things, but finally this is a bondage we have brought upon ourselves, a bondage from which Christ sets us free. God is creator and lord over us, but God's lordship

does not turn us into mere puppets. Human decision is an important factor in the world. Although the freedom of which Christians speak is primarily the freedom we have in Christ, this does not mean that there are any human beings who are mere automatons. Nor does it mean that in fact the believer is free from all bondage. In Metz's view: 'Transcendence occurs in an "ec-stasis" in which man momentarily moves beyond ... without, however, ever completely escaping the horizon of shared being in a finite world.'[36]

There has been a confusing history of interaction between theological reflections about freedom and philosophical ones. The idea of freedom has proved quite baffling to philosophy, because human reason is prone to posit causes antecedent to every effect as the adequate explanation of that effect. The preceding chapter offered an account of how Whitehead locates an element of decision in every occasion of experience and shows how that is an act of transcending the given world. The ontological fact of freedom is the context within which the more specifically theological talk of bondage as well as of freedom makes sense.

Apart from this transcending, the other features of the human situation make no sense. The intrinsic value of each experience cannot be separated from the element of freedom through which it realises itself. Our interconnectedness with one another is not merely a given but also a set of relations that we can weaken or strengthen. It is by virtue of transcending that we can see the community of interests that we share with others and convert apparent trade-offs into mutually supportive goods.

Marxist theory does not exclude freedom in this sense. Its ultimate goal is for universal human freedom. But in its analysis of the past and present it stresses the conditionedness of thought and action by economic interests almost to the exclusion of the recognition of the universal presence of transcending. Marxists tend to see transcending only in science and especially in their own science. The party, informed by this science, understands itself as the enlightened vanguard of an otherwise blind proletariat. Partly as a result of this theory, many Marxists have felt little need to respect the opinions and concerns of those who, as they see it, reflect interests that block the realisation of the true goal.

It is the merit of liberal thought to have taken human freedom much more seriously. Instead of engineering people into achieving what the elite believes is good for them, liberal political theory encourages wide participation in shaping and reshaping the goals to be attained. Institutions have been developed which have had some success in forcing those in power to respect the freedom of ordinary people. One major and legitimate reason for Christian support of liberalism is that liberal thought in this respect corresponds more closely with Christian belief.

But the Christian understanding of freedom cannot be separated from the understanding of bondage. We are free, but our freedom is severely limited. In Whitehead's vision we are free to constitute ourselves out of our world, but what the world is, out of which we constitute ourselves, is given. We transcend that world, so that we are responsible for what we make of ourselves, but in the transcending we are still chiefly shaped by what we transcend. Marxists are largely correct in supposing that our beliefs on many subjects can be viewed as ideology designed to support and disguise our class interests. We pretend to much more independence and objectivity of judgment than we exemplify.

The practical limitations of liberal democracy arise in part from these limits to our freedom. Instead of a community of people exercising wise judgements about the general welfare or even acting out of enlightened self-interest, we have large groups of people expressing unexamined prejudices which are all too easily manipulated by those who control the mass media. Democracies can only survive through checks and balances which reduce the danger of disastrous actions expressive of mass prejudices. They have succeeded in maintaining institutions which allow the element of transcending that really does characterise all people to have some measure of effectiveness while at the same time adjusting to the bondage under which we all labour.

But the Marxist critique still applies to democratic institutions. They have not learned how to give voice to the more disadvantaged segments of the society. To make effective use of democratic institutions requires education and a measure of wealth. Those who lack these requisites are likely to have only the appearance of participation. Only as democratic institutions succeed in transforming themselves in the light of the Marxist critique can they realise their own intentions and continue to deserve Christian support. This has, of course, been the programme of many social democrats.

Liberal theory tends to use double images of human beings. There is *homo economicus*, on the one hand, who rationally calculates private economic advantage. Then there is another kind of rationality required of public *servants* who are to be dedicated to the common good. They are expected to engage in planning for the public welfare in a way that is not affected by their private interests. In this they are to be supported by neutral and objective scientists who provide them with the information they need. There are, of course, no purely self-interested persons on the one side nor any who can ever free themselves from self-interest on the other. Both abstractions are serious distortions. And both interfere with realistic expectations of political processes. A model of very limited, but never negligible, transcending, varying in degree from time to time and person to person, can provide a more realistic approach to the political world. Reinhold Niebuhr contributed extensively to the appropriate type of Christian reflection.

Marxist theory has the same duality of images, with still greater danger that they be applied to different segments of the community. The masters of Marxist science understand themselves to transcend their personal and economic interests radically, whereas those who are not masters are caught up in the laws which the science describes. Hence great confidence is placed in the planning for the many by the few. The results have at times been appalling. In the course of time Communist countries have learned that the Marxist elite is not free from all distorting bondage. In Yugoslavia we have a Communist country which is experimenting with trusting ordinary people with far more power to make decisions.

(4) Most Christians have believed that our calling can never be fully captured in any rational or ethical system. That is, we are called to obey God or to accept the guidance of the Holy Spirit even beyond our ability to calculate that a particular action will yield the best results or that it conforms to a valid principle. That does not mean that either teleological or deontological principles can be dismissed. They are certainly useful to Christians and function as an important check against the abuses of the understanding of our immediacy to God. But Christians have also tried to guard against the identification of the Christian life with the ethical life as that can be defined by rational ethical principles. In political theology this is often done by emphasising the futurity of God.

Metz puts human responsibility 'in the new perspective of the full horizon of God's future intention for the world'.[37]

In previous chapters I have explained how both Wieman and Whitehead have clarified this situation. For Wieman any ethical principle to which I now adhere is a created good rather than the creative good. To serve the creative good means to allow even that principle, however worthy it may be, to be transformed in unforeseeable ways. For Whitehead the contrast is between the new aim derived from God in each moment and all that is inherited from the past. What is inherited includes ethical principles. The new aim is relevant to that inheritance, but it is not derived from it, and in some measure the aim will transcend mere conformity to the inheritance. Hence for both Wieman and Whitehead the appropriate stance of the believer is finally trust in the unforeseeable call of God rather than conformation to a pre-established understanding of the content of that call.

However, neither Wieman nor Whitehead understands this confidence in God to be a blind waiting for mysterious messages. On the contrary, it is the openness to let a certain type of process work in us, one that can be described on the basis of what has been observed in the previous working of God. For both Wieman and Whitehead this process is creative unification of a multiplicity of elements into a new whole.

In describing this process both Wieman and Whitehead are dealing with individual human experiences. Hence the meaning of what is said can be illustrated by an ordinary example from human experience. When one listens to a good lecture some of the ideas there offered are different from those which one had in advance. Otherwise one would be bored indeed! There are several ways one can respond to such different ideas. One can ignore them or quickly forget them. One can reject them. One can replace previous ideas with them. One can add them to one's present stock of ideas. These responses may all be justified at various times and places. But none of them are creative. The other option is that one can integrate aspects of what is heard with what one has previously believed in a way that leads to a position that takes account of both. That can only happen if one thinks new thoughts. In Whitehead's language one would then have converted the multiplicity of ideas into a contrast through which their distinct integrity is maintained in a unity that differs from all of them. Readiness to have one's thinking transformed in this way is openness to God's gift of the new.

This seems far removed from the political sphere, and there is no one-to-one connection between this view of openness to God, on the one hand, and a particular understanding of political norms on the other. Yet there is an important relationship. Political life also is concerned with teleological and deontological principles, and rightly so. But a government which guides itself by viewing the present action only as a means to a better future is not likely to achieve the better future, and the attempt to act by principles alone often becomes seriously inhumane. Political theory needs to deal as much or more with the question of the type of social change that is itself healthy as with the question of the goal that is being sought through such changes or the principles to which one supposes changes should conform.

There have been a variety of ideas about the nature of desirable change that have influenced political thinking in the past. To remain in the sphere of the practical, consider the alternatives that have faced many non-Western countries in the twentieth century. Such a country might try to ignore or reject Western culture and technology, but that has proved difficult if not impossible. At the opposite extreme it could try to replace traditional culture with a new one. The Red Guards seem to have attempted something like that in China. A nation may try to add some features of Western culture and technology to its previous patterns without altering these. For example a Westernised urban elite may rule over a traditional rural society without encouraging any changes in that society.

Hegel's dialectic has provided a much more profound way of viewing social change. A particular form of society may generate forces opposed to it which then overthrow it. In this process some of the values of the overthrown society are lost. But in the end these values can be recovered in a further development of the new society into a synthesis of both. In a Marxist version this means that capitalist society generates an alienated proletariat. The overthrow of the capitalist society by the proletariat involves the destruction of the personal liberties that were enjoyed by the bourgeoisie. But once the proletariat is fully established it develops into a classless society in which these liberties and more are enjoyed by all.

Process theology need not deny that this kind of dialectic can be found in history, but its occurrence seems to be a contingent matter. There is no assurance, built into the process, of a fortunate outcome. The destruction of one good for the sake of another may lead to the permanent loss of the former rather than to its recovery in a higher synthesis. The more thoroughly this good is extirpated, the greater the danger that it will not be renewed, whereas Marxist theory may encourage zealots, as in Campuchea, to suppose that the more fully they destroy the society they encounter the sooner the perfected society can be built.

Hence process theology favours, also on the political scale, the transformation of differences into contrasts. That means that diverse interests and ideals are to be united in higher syntheses in the present. If Western culture and technology are to be introduced, their synthesis with existing patterns is a matter of present importance. The aim must be a progressive creative transformation of society. No blueprint for the desired result can be developed in advance, but it will be possible to judge as time goes on whether in fact the best in the existing culture is being effectively integrated with the best in Western culture. If so, the pattern of development can be adjudged as healthy.

To say this is to take sides in a contemporary debate within Christian ethics in favour of the primacy and ultimacy of reconciliation. But this must not be done without full appreciation of the stance of those who point out, quite rightly, that when masses of people are powerless they cannot be reconciled with their oppressors. Reconciliation presupposes relative equality on the part of the forces or ideas that are to be reconciled. The goal of reconciliation may, for long periods of time, require Christians to throw their support fully on the side of the weaker party.

Still there is a difference between doing this for the sake of ultimate reconciliation and for the sake of revolutionary negation. One may throw one's support on one side while inwardly appreciating what is positive in the other. The goal one tries to hold before both parties can be a creative synthesis of their aspirations. Destructive violence is not wholly precluded, but its justification must be its contribution to reconciliation. Judged in this way its use will be rarer than when one views negation dialectically as the road to synthesis.

(5) Although the history of Christianity is replete with instances of the use of violence, and although this violence has often been employed for destruction of the enemy rather than reconciliation, dominant Christian teaching has nevertheless encouraged respect for the human integrity and worth of all people and has viewed violence against persons as undesirable. If violence is to be used at all, it is as a last resort. It is far better to win the hearts of people than to compel them to outward conformity to Christian teaching which they do not inwardly accept. Preaching is the proper modality of the church's extension of its influence rather than military or legal coercion. For Metz, too, the Christian advocacy of love involves a sustained critique of coercive power.[38] Christian 'praxis cannot lead to an abstract or a violent negation of the individual'.[39]

Since no society can exist without some measure of coercion as well as some measure of persuasion, Christian teaching on the proper relation of these two forms of power has been complex and diverse. Whitehead's thought stands in the mainstream of this tradition of reflection about power. There is no question for him of the massive importance of the coercive elements in any society. But the success of a society is to be measured by the extent to which persuasive factors operate within it. After a rich discussion of the interweaving of coercive and persuasive factors in society, Whitehead summarises his position as follows:

> First, there stands the inexorable law that apart from some transcendent aim the civilized life either wallows in pleasure or relapses slowly into a barren repetition with waning intensities of feeling. Secondly, there stands the iron cumpulsion of nature that the bodily necessities of food, clothing, and shelter be provided. The rigid limits which are thereby set to modes of social existence can only be mitigated by the growth of an understanding by which the interplay between man and the rest of nature can be adjusted. Thirdly, the compulsory dominance of men over men has a double significance. It has a benign effect so far as it secures the coordination of behavior necessary for social welfare. But it is fatal to extend this dominion beyond the barest limits necessary for this coordination. The progressive societies are those which most decisively have trusted themselves to the fourth factor which is the way of persuasion. Amidst all the activities of mankind there are three which chiefly have promoted this last factor in human life. They are family affections aroused in sex relations and in the nurture of children, intellectural curiosity leading to enjoyment in the interchange of ideas, and — as soon as large-scale societies arose — the practice of Commerce.

But beyond these special activities a greater bond of sympathy has arisen. This bond is the growth of reverence for that power in virtue of which nature harbours ideal ends, and produces individual beings capable of conscious discrimination of such ends. This reverence is the foundation of the respect for man as man. It thereby secures that liberty of thought and action, required for the upward adventure of life on this earth.[40]

Whitehead here recognises the inevitability of compulsion, but his point is that in the healthy society force is minimised. The problem is that in so many actual societies violent compulsion by the state vastly exceeds acceptable limits and is structurally institutionalised. Christians must then wrestle with the issue of using revolutionary violence to overthrow the institutionalised violence of oppressive regimes. In Nicaragua the Christian conscience sided with the use of relatively limited violence to bring an end to massive structural violence by a corrupt dictatorship. Thus far the new government has shown itself able to rule largely by persuasion. This is surely a gain worth the price paid.

The preference of process theology for the extension of the role of persuasion is not *ad hoc*. It arises directly out of principles already enunciated. It is by persuasion that we respect the freedom of those whom we would influence. It is persuasion that introduces the possibility of creative synthesis of the new with the old which is the mark of healthy development or growth. Beyond this, process theology grounds the perference for persuasion in its understanding of God's relation to the world. To some extent this can be said for all Christian theology, but many theologies have attributed to God coercive as well as persuasive agency. This has led to expectations that God will save us from natural catastrophes and the horrors of history — expectations which are repeatedly frustrated. It has led to insoluble formulations of the problem of theodicy. And it has at times let Christians themselves to adopt coercive measures in supposed imitation of God. Process theology believes that God's power should be seen more consistently in the light of the cross, but it does not see this as weakness. The only power that is truly creative is persuasive power, and this power is exercised in supreme and ultimate fashion by God. All the persuasive power that operates in the universe derives from God, and that means that all truly creative activity derives from God. If we would be perfect as God is perfect, then we will undertake vigorously to affect the course of events creatively, and that means by persuasion. We will construct institutions that encourage persuasive relationships and provide a context in which the possibility of such relationships is safeguarded. We will also realise that this entails the construction of a society in which the natural necessities of life are provided for all as easily and freely as possible so that the needs of survival will not dominate human activity.

NOTES

1   Helmut Gollwitzer, *Forderungen der Umkehr: Beiträge zur Gesellschaft* (Munich: Christian Kaiser Verlag, 1976), p. 173. (My translation.)

2   See his 1919 address on 'The Christian's place in society'. This is chapter VIII in Karl Barth, *The Word of God and the Word of Man*, trans. Douglass Horton (New York: Harper & Bros., 1928).

3   Paul Tillich and Carl Richard Wegener, 'Der Sozialismus als Kirchenfrage', in Paul Tillich, *Gesammelte Werke*, vol. 2 (Stuttgart: Evangelisches Verlagswerk, 1962), p. 19. For this reference I am indebted to John R. Stumme's introduction to Paul Tillich, *The Socialist Decision*, trans. Franklin Sherman (New York: Harper & Row, 1977), p. xii.

4   Tillich, *The Socialist Decision*, p. 161.

5   Gollwitzer, p. 162. (My translation.)

6   Wolfhart Pannenberg, 'Der Sozialismus – das wahre Gottesreich?', in Wolfhart Teichert, ed., *Müssen Christen Sozialisten Sein? Zwischen Glaube und Politik* (Hamburg: Lutherisches Verlagshaus, 1976) p. 60. (My translation.)

7   *Ibid.*, p. 64. (My translation.)

8   The documents associated with this event are available in John Eagleson, ed., *Christians and Socialism*, trans. John Drury (Maryknoll, N.Y.: Orbis Books, 1975).

9   I owe these quotations, as well as examples in the preceding paragraph, to John C. Bennett, 'Religious faith and political participation', written for the 10–11 April 1981, meeting of the Pacific Coast Theological Group.

10 Johann Baptist Metz, 'Political theology', in *Sacramentum Mundi*, vol. 5, p. 37.

11 Johann Baptist Metz, *Theology of the World*, trans. William Glen-Doepel (New York: Herder and Herder, 1971), p. 107.

12 Metz, 'Political theology', p. 37.

13 *Ibid.*

14 Metz, *Theology of the World*, pp. 122–3.

15 Johann Baptist Metz and Jean-Pierre Jossua, ed., *Christianity and Socialism*, (New York: Seabury Press, 1977), p. viii.

16 Dorethee Sölle, *Political Theology*, trans. John Shelley (Philadelphia, Pa.: Fortress Press, 1971), pp. 58–9.

17 *Ibid.*, p. 77.

18 *Ibid.*, p. 76.

19 See *Beyond Mere Dialogue: On Being Christian and Socialist*. (Detroit, Mich.: American Christians Toward Socialism, 1978).

20 Jürgen Moltmann, *The Crucified God*, trans. R. A. Wilson and John Bowden (New York: Harper & Row, 1974), pp. 332–5.

21 Jürgen Moltmann, 'An open letter to Jose Miguez Bonino', *Christianity and Crisis* (29 March 1976), p. 60.

22 By 'the people' Moltmann means those who are ruled. He points out that the claim to liberate the people was made by Mussolini and Hitler. He warns that ' "socialism *for* the people" turns out to be either doctrinaire or bureaucratic oppression of the people. True socialism is "socialism *of* the people" '. Jürgen Moltmann, 'Hope in the struggle of the people', *Christianity and Crisis* (21 March 1977), p. 52.

23 Moltmann, 'An open letter', p. 61.

24 *Ibid.*, p. 62.

25 Frederick Lawrence argues that political theology in general and Metz in particular need to engage political theory much more intensively. I share the view that more needs to be done — much more than I have suggested in what follows. 'Political theology and the "Longer cycle of decline" ', in *Lonergan Workshop*, vol. I., ed. Fred Lawrence (Missoula, Mont.: Scholars Press, 1978), pp. 235f.

26 Metz, *Theology of the World*, pp. 117–18.

27 Peter F. Drucker, *Management: Tasks, Responsibilities, Practices* (New York: Harper & Row, 1973), p. 181.

28 Harry Braverman, *Labor and Monopoly Capital* (New York: Monthly Review Press, 1974), p. 88.

29 Jeremy Rifkin with Ted Howard, *The Emerging Order: God in the Age of Scarcity* (New York: G. P. Putnam's Sons, 1979), p. 189.

30 Robert Heilbroner, *The Great Ascent: the Struggle for Economic Development in our Time* (New York: Harper & Row, 1963), p. 137.

31 Lester Brown, *The Twenty-Ninth Day: Accommodating Human Needs and Numbers to the Earth's Resources* (New York: W. W. Norton & Co., Inc., 1978), pp. 302–3.

32 The requirements for efficiency are discussed at length and with many examples by Peter F. Drucker in the book cited in Note 27. He shows how participation in the making of decisions, feedback information on how the worker is doing, and continuous learning jointly constitute optimum conditions. Clearly these are conditions which are satisfying to the worker as well. See especially chapter 21.

33 Roger Dick Johns, *Man in the World: the Political Theology of Johannes Baptist Metz* (Missoula, Mont.: Scholars Press, 1976), p. 80.

34 Arthur K. Okun, *Equality and Efficiency: the Big Tradeoff* (Washington, D.C.: The Brookings Institute, 1975).

35   Amory B. Lovins, *Soft Energy Paths: Toward a Durable Peace* (Cambridge, Mass.: Ballinger Publishing Co., 1977).

36   Johns, *Man in the World*, p. 80.

37   *Ibid.*, p. 90.

38   Metz, *Theology of the World*, p. 119.

39   Johann Baptist Metz, *Faith in History and Society: Toward a Practical Fundamental Theology*, trans. David Smith (New York: Seabury Press, 1980), p. 56.

40   Alfred North Whitehead, *Adventures of Ideas* (New York: The Free Press, 1933), pp. 108–9.

41   The pattern in this section of formulating Christian principles by which both capitalist and Marxist theory and practice are to be judged parallels the work of Peter Berger in *Pyramids of Sacrifice: Political Ethics and Social Change* (New York: Basic Books, 1974). Berger shows the horrendous consequences of capitalist ideology in Brazil and of Marxist ideology in China. He concludes not that capitalism and Marxism are thereby totally invalidated but that standards of humane practice must be employed in evaluating each instance in which they are applied. 'Brazil does not exhaust the possibilities of capitalism, and there are socialist possibilities beyond Marxist China. It is the quest of such other possibilities that should preoccupy anyone concerned with the mitigation of human suffering in the course of social change' (p. 163). I suggest that Japan and Cuba provide far more positive models of capitalism and socialism at work.

Chapter Six

SOCIOLOGICAL THEOLOGY
OR ECOLOGICAL THEOLOGY

When political theology was launched in the mid-sixties there were questions about the scope of the word political. But the inherent tendency of the term to focus only on the human occasioned no comment. At that time few were raising questions about the other creatures with whom human beings share this planet. When Dorothee Sölle wrote in 1971 of the indivisible salvation of the whole world, she and her readers assumed without reflection that the whole world is the world of human beings.[1] But as the seventies progressed and the environmental crisis forced itself on public attention, more and more Christians became troubled about the separation of humanity from the rest of nature. At that point the adequacy of a political theology came under question from a new point of view.

Moltmann quickly recognised the importance of the new range of issues and incorporated them into his theology. The quotation from *The Crucified God* in Chapter Five shows how fully and profoundly he did so. He presented nature not simply in terms of its appearance and utility to human beings but as having 'its own rights and equilibria'.[2] The passage is in the chapter entitled 'Ways towards the political liberation of man', which suggests that Moltmann had no problem extending his already broad use of 'political' to include the ecological as well. This may reflect the fact that the category *political theology*, has not been the major one under which Moltmann has done his work. For him the political is a theme and horizon along-side others in the general context of a theology of the cross and of hope.

For process theologians the ecological horizon is even more

important than for Moltmann, and the question arises whether this excludes us from political theology. Metz, the central representative of political theology, seems to resist this enlargement of the horizons. This chapter is primarily a conversation with Metz on this topic. In so far as the inclusion of ecological theology in political theology is a terminological problem, it is not debated. The argument is that the ecological horizon is needed if we truly care about the indivisible salvation of the whole world. The claim, therefore, is that ecological theology is the appropriate fulfilment of the intentions of political theology.

Section I describes the influence of Kant upon Metz and upon his anthropocentric understanding of political theology. With this it contrasts the philosophy of Whitehead and its different implications. In Section II this contrast is further developed at the level of practice. It is argued that the anthropocentric vision has led and continues to lead in self-defeating directions. Section III shows that without altogether ceasing to be anthropocentric sociological theory can become much more sensitive to ecological issues and that ecological theology needs to be informed by sociological understanding. Although in this way the initial oppositions can be extensively reduced, a difference remains.

I

Metz is not, of course, ignorant of the environmental problems which we face. He acknowledges them once in *Faith in History and Society*. But he does so primarily in order to insist that they do not justify a shift of hirozons from history to nature. He writes:

> As soon ... as the problems of the preservation of the environment, the safeguarding of the sources of raw materials and an enlightened attitude towards the future are taken seriously, it becomes clear that history cannot be supported by a theory of nature, but that, on the contrary, nature must be safeguarded by a reflection about our historical responsibility for nature, so that it is not exploited without restraint. It also becomes apparent how far-reaching the effects are of an understanding that politics are the new name for civilization, since, if we regard it as an essential task to preserve nature as a pre-condition for a rational future, then civilization will justify both its original name and its claim to be able to overcome barbarism. The category of responsibility for one's own actions, for others and for nature clearly demonstrates that

civilization must justify itself in politics. In this way, the species becomes conscious of its own original process of life. This consciousness makes it possible for us to understand the unity of reason and reality as the reconciliation between nature and history.[3]

There is an obvious truth to Metz's point. What we need is responsible human action in relation to our environment. But the way Metz makes this point reflects a view that is very different from that of Moltmann and process theology. For Metz the rest of creation can appear only in the horizon of history. It is not a topic of reflection except in its relation to human beings. And in that relation it is immediately taken up into the framework of human activity.

This subsumption of nature under history is not a casual matter. It expresses Metz's philosophical views as carefully worked out in *Christliche Anthropozentrik*. In order to understand what Metz means by political theology, and thus the obstacle to a process theologian's becoming a political theologian in Metz's sense, we will need to study more carefully the position to which he came in that book.

The transcendental Thomism of Metz's teachers was dependent on the influence of Kant and on the fresh reading of Thomas which the study of Kant made possible. Kant's great contribution was to argue that the world as it is in itself is completely unknowable. What we perceive and reflect about are the phenomena, that is, the appearances of the world. Those appearances, which are the only world we have, are structured by human mind. They do not in themselves possess even spatial and temporal character. These are imposed upon them by mind. And although Kant's own formulations suggest that the occurrence of the phenomena is the result of the interaction of mind with the world of things in themselves, his followers abandoned talk of such a completely unknowable world. In the tradition of German idealism, the world *is* the human world, that is, mind.

Metz conceived only one fundamental alternative to this anthropocentric position. That is the cosmological view which understands reality in terms of nature, i.e., what is given objectively in human experience. The Greeks understood human beings as part of such a nature.

With these alternatives in mind Metz examined Thomas. He came quickly to the conclusion that Thomas cannot be read as an objective, cosmological thinker. Thomas was aware of human beings as subjects and understood both world and God from the point of view of human subjectivity. Perceiving Thomas in this way, Metz finds that 'the worldliness of the world is not therefore originally conceived in a cosmocentric way as an already given, self-contained, and actual existent, which man encounters'.[4] 'Human existence — that is: ecstatic subjectivity; both — man and world — are synthesized apriori in the one being of man.'[5] 'Man is not real because he appears in a real world, but the world is real, because man in his being really stands overagainst himself as real, because he exists ecstatically.'[6]

This basic philosophical understanding is consistently expressed in Metz's later work. In an unpublished lecture presented in Barcelona in 1966 'he divides the history of philosophy of religion into two periods: the development of faith within the horizon of nature and within the horizon of history'. The former he calls metaphysics, which he defines as 'a conceptualizing understanding of the totality within the horizon of nature'. This metaphysic 'has wrecked itself against the problem of history'.[7] From the historical point of view nature is seen as 'the world surrounding man's activity, standing at his disposal and subject to his alterations'.[8]

Although there are distinctive features in this appropriation of Kant, they are not of primary importance for Metz's view of the natural world. His important original contribution came slightly later in his revisions of Rahner's writings. There he began increasingly to emphasise the social character of human existence. This is fully expressed in his article on *Mitsein* in the *Lexikon für Theologie und Kirche*:

> Man already gains entrance into the reality of his worldly—corporal being in shared existence with other ontologically equal subjects. He encounters the remainder of what exists in the world (that which is present at hand as a thing) within the horizon of this fundamental, shared existence. 'World' itself is to be understood 'anthropocentrically,' i.e., as always mediated through shared existence. One's own being and shared existence form the one, continual, whole structure of the material worldly being of man. In the self-understanding of man the other person is already co-understood; in his self-fulfillment the other person is already co-determined. The more radical this self-fulfillment is, the more universal is the existential pre-forming of the space of this fulfillment, the 'world' of the other.[9]

This shift from a focus on the individual to the emphasis on the social is crucial for the emergence of political theology, but it does not affect the understanding of the natural world. Human beings are now collectively contrasted with the remainder of what exists, and this is all understood as what is present at hand as a thing. Hence Metz's philosophy precludes his moving with Moltmann to consideration of nature as having its own rights and equilibrium.

Whitehead rejects both of the basic options between which Metz makes his choice. To interpret the human subject as merely an objective part of a purely objective world is completely unacceptable. But to see the toatlity of nature as existing only in and through the being of human beings is equally unacceptable. Whitehead agrees with Metz that apart from subjectivity there can be nothing at all, but he does not agree that apart from *human* subjectivity there can be nothing at all. Apart from human subjectivity, for example, there can be the subjectivity of a chimpanzee.

To extend subjectivity to chimpanzees, in itself, would not alter the structure of Metz's thought very much. But of course the chimpanzee is only illustrative of the point that subjectivity need not be defined as human subjectivity. No doubt there are features of human subjectivity not shared by any other creature, but many of these are not shared with all other human beings either. We must avoid defining the subjectivity that is the requisite for reality too elaborately! What we know of biological evolution suggests that modern human subjectivity emerged very gradually over a long period of time out of simpler forms of subjectivity. There is no indication that the world came into being abruptly with the appearance of advanced human subjectivity!

There is a problem also with the relation of subjectivity to our notions of self-consciousness, consciousness and subconscious experience. Metz does not tell us where he draws the line. For Whitehead no sharp line is to be drawn. Even unconscious experience has its element of subjectivity. And indeed for billions of years after the Big Bang there was probably no other kind. When we think of such a world we should not conceive of it visually, for that visual world did not exist. Indeed, most of the phenomena which constitute the Kantian world did not exist. They came into being correlatively with animals with elaborate nervous systems, and some of them awaited the arrival of human beings. But that does not mean that there was then no world at all.

Metz speaks of our shared existence with other people. That

corresponds with Whitehead's understanding also. Our existence is constituted by the participation of others in it. There is no purely individual existence which then subsequently comes to be shared. But Whitehead does not agree that there is a radical difference between our relations with other human beings and with the rest of the world. We have shared existence with all other creatures. Of course there *are* differences. But these differences do not warrant viewing everything that is not human as mere things at the disposal of human beings.

The central notion by which Whitehead understands this sharing of entities in one another is 'prehension'. The best place to look in experience to identify a prehension is in the way in which experience of one moment flows into the next. I am always aware of being continuous with what I have been just before. The emotions of the immediate past, for example, perpetuate themselves into the present. Also I find myself completing a word which I began a moment ago. What I now am is largely constituted by the presence within me of what I was just before. 'Prehension' is Whitehead's term for the way in which the present experience includes, and thereby takes account of, past experience.

Present experience is taking account of much else besides the immediately past personal experiences that flow into it. Especially what is happening throughout the body is impressing itself upon present experience. I feel the discomfort in my back or the sensuous enjoyment in my hand. These too are prehensions. Then there is much taking place in my body which affects my experience without my awareness. For example, I am never aware of events in my brain, and yet these have an immediate bearing upon the content of experience. These too are prehended. My actual experience is a prehensive unification of my past experiences and what is taking place in my body. Through my body I am prehending also the events in the wider world. Thus we are not related to other people in one way and to everything else in another. All relations are prehensions, and all prehensions bring what is there into the presently self-constituting subjective immediacy.

My prehensive unification is partly conscious, certainly not entirely so. In the case of one of the cells in my finger, it is probably not conscious at all. But in both cases the prehensive unifications, what Whitehead calls the actual occasions of experience, are highly selective unifications of other prehensive unifications, conscious or not. There is nothing actual to prehend other than such acts of unification.

Human beings also present to themselves through their eyes and ears and other sense organs a world of phenomena. These seem to be given as mere objects, mere things, and it was interpreting the world in terms of such objects, especially of vision, that led to the objectifying cosmologies of which Metz is rightly critical. The world of prehensive unifications is badly misinterpreted when we take our categories from the world of visual objects. Physics has already learned that it cannot understand its subatomic particles by categories drawn from the visual world. Philosophers and religious people have long known that human beings cannot be understood this way. It is time to realise that this objectifying knowledge, while useful for many practical purposes, distorts all reality.

II

It seemed necessary to bring out clearly the philosophical differences between Kantians and Whiteheadians which underly our disagreements as to what political theology should be. But this is not the place for a philosophical debate. The concern of this chapter is practice. To a process theologian it appears that the practice encouraged by Kantian philosophy has been disastrous so far as the human relation to the remainder of the created order is concerned. Some of the disasters could be avoided without altering the basic philosophic view, but such *ad hoc* improvements in practice are not sufficient. The kind of anthropocentricity established by Kant and affirmed by Metz is, in process perspective, an important part of the problem. If theology is 'political' only when it accepts these parameters, then process theologians do not want to become political theologians.

However, if political theology at bottom is theology directed by commitment to the indivisible salvation of the whole world, it in no way entails a non-ecological attitude or indifference to other creatures. On the contrary, in Moltmann political theology has already in part become ecological theology. The form of political theology to which a process theologian can aspire is a thoroughly ecological theology.

For process theology, as an ecological theology, human beings are part of nature. We are a very special part with peculiar capacities and value. But we came into being at a late point in the evolutionary process and we will some day be gone. That will not be the end of the world, only of humanity. Viewing ourselves in this way it is natural to ask the question of what our prospects for survival may be. We see that other species are becoming extinct at a rapid rate,[10] and we find no reason that extinction should not be our fate as well. Indeed, we see that the degradation of the environment led to the downfall of many ancient civilisations, and that we are now engaged in such a degradation on a global scale. 'The human prospect', to use a phrase from the title of Heilbroner's book,[11] is bleak.

Viewing our species from the point of view of the total natural process does not mean adopting an attitude of calm detachment. On the contrary, we who do so are in danger of becoming shrill, especially when our fellows turn a deaf ear to our warnings. For us it seems supremely important to develop national and global policies which will reverse our headlong race toward suicide. The piecemeal approach to a few of the sociologically understandable and manageable problems, which is favoured by so many, seems woefully inadequate to stem the tidal wave of destruction.

The threat is not from ecological deterioration alone. On the contrary, there is a much more imminent threat of human self-destruction through nuclear war. As pressures on resources and accompanying economic difficulties grow worse, the likelihood that all nations with nuclear potential will refrain from using their power grows less. Once a nuclear war begins there is great danger that it will not be contained. The combination of the ecological and nuclear threats leads to what is in the most straightforward sense a threat to the survival of the human race. Nothing appears more important than so altering the course of human action as to make this total destruction less likely.

How, then, does this appear to Kantian eyes? The first answer must be that there is a striking absence of discussion of the threat to human survival among philosophers and theologians heavily influenced by Kant. This is not surprising. Logically, from the point of view of this philosophy the end of the human race is the end of being as such. This is a difficult thought — one that falls outside the system. This does not necessarily mean that Kantians deny the possibility or likelihood of such an end. But the practical result is silence. They simply do not discuss it.

It might seem that in the case of those who direct our attention dominantly to the future, the threat of human self-destruction would play a central role. But here too there is silence. The topic does not arise directly in Metz's book of 1977. It may be that his reflections about the evil of the evolutionary viewpoint and the desirability of renewing the apocalyptic one constitute his reaction to what others are saying about the threat. The fact that he leaves open the possibility of failure for the Christian enterprise also suggests that he does not ignore it. But it is significant that an entire book could be written in 1977 about the practical meaning of a theology of hope without discussing the relevance to that practical meaning of the serious doubtfulness of human survival. One must judge that this topic is not readily assimilated into the Kantian frame of reference. That seems to the outsider to be systematically the case.

Metz did deal with the 'crisis of survival' in an address to the Evangelischen Kirchentag in Nürnberg in 1979. This lecture shows far more sensitivity to ecological concerns than his earlier writings had. Indeed from the point of view of an ecological theologian it is an excellent statement. It may indicate that the problem felt in identifying an ecologically sensitive theology as a political theology will soon be resolved. But with respect to the question of survival it is noteworthy that Metz speaks of the 'so-called crisis of survival'. He calls for a revolution of human attitudes toward nature and even more toward other human beings. His strongest statement is: 'I cannot see how, without such a revolution, a way out of this crisis of survival that does not involve some kind of catastrophe is possible at all'.[12] One does not sense that Metz seriously reckons with the possibility that the human race will not survive.

There is, of course, no special virtue in harping on this danger. But our attitudes and our practice will be different according to whether we take it seriously or whether we always translate the crisis of survival into the urgent need for an anthropological revolution. Adherence to the Kantian philosophy almost necessitates this type of translation. But we are not likely to forestall an end of history if we are not able to face its likelihood squarely and discuss it directly. If political theology cannot deal openly with this topic, then a process theologian does not want to become a political theologian. But it is arbitrary to limit political theology to the sphere of Kantian hegemony.

The absolutisation of history and the ignoring of the effects of a real nature upon historical events has had other negative consequences against which Kantian theology does little to protect us. History means primarily civilisation, as Metz sees when he says that politics is the new name for civilisation. Both 'politics' and 'civilisation' point to the city, and in fact the movement of civilisation is toward urbanisation and industrialisation. Unconsciously, perhaps, the subsistence farmer, and even the peasant village, are assimilated to images of an unhistorical nature which serves civilisation and industrialisation but has no inherent reality. After all, history and sociology are written by urban people. Rural areas are viewed as remote and backward. Primitive cultures are studied by anthropology, not sociology. History belongs to the city.

This deep-seated perspective has had profound consequences for development policy since World War II. Development is judged largely in terms of GNP, which is a measure of goods and services that are exchanged for money in the market-place. Subsistence farming, accordingly, is hardly considered a significant economic activity. Employment is understood as working for wages, and since subsistence farmers do not receive wages they are not considered among the employed. A report of the U.S. Department of Labor declared that only 5 percent of the women of Africa work. Irene Tinker comments: 'This clearly is an absurd assertion about a continent where women are reported to be doing 60–80 percent of the work in the fields and working up to 16 hours a day during the planting season.'[13] A goal of development is to draw people into the money economy despite the often negative consequences on food production and family life. Until they are part of the national economic system, they are simply invisible – just a part of that nature which is the backdrop for history.

In our eagerness to draw people into history thus defined, development policies have encouraged the shift from raising food for local consumption to growing cash crops for export. Often this has meant the destruction of the family farm in favour of great plantations commercially operated by foreign corporations. When the problems of increasing food production is addressed, industrial methods are applied, as in the 'green revolution', further supporting the concentration of land ownership in a few hands. This has often meant the end of a sustainable agriculture in favour of one that rapidly depletes the soil and hastens desertification. Production depends on expensive machinery, oil, and chemical fertilisers, not available to subsistence farmers. But all this is not too high a price to pay if cash can be raised for industrial development in the cities! There is where 'history' really happens. The result of such views, of course, is that few of the so-called developing countries can any longer feed themselves! Malnutrition and even starvation are rampant, the soil base for feeding future generations is rapidly eroded, and the social and cultural fabric is torn. All this — because the 'reality' is 'history' and not 'nature'. Even now the problem of developing a sustainable agriculture in order that future generations may eat does not grip the mind as does the problem of justice for the urban poor. It seems to fall outside of the categories of the Kantian imagination.

This is not at all to suggest that a Kantian theologian such as Metz lacks deep concern for the Third World. He desires for that world freedom and justice. These are noble ideals, and the willingness to give of oneself generously that they may be realised is indeed commendable. The problem is that without a wider perspective the policies one supports for the sake of freedom and justice can sometimes be ambiguous in their consequences or even harmful.

Out of a concern for justice, people often quote figures showing the gross disparity in the per capita GNP of different countries. The apparent implication is that justice requires reduction of the disparity. Such reduction requires rapid industrialisation on the part of the poorer country. Hence our moral task is defined as transferring technology and funding industrial expansion. Yet it may be that this whole 'development' is destructive. The need may be for simple improvements in farming implements and seeds for subsistence farmers along with aid to peasant villages for improved hygiene and reforestation of their hills. When these are neglected and money is pumped instead into industrial development, the males move to the cities, destroying the communities which have sustained the people for thousands of years and creating huge urban slums. Policies that would bring dignity and significant improvement to peasant life would do little for the GNP, but they might do much more than new factories for the indivisible salvation of the whole world. Preoccupation with 'history' in its opposition to 'nature' largely obscures this possibility.

The topic of limits is another on which ecological theology perceives the requirements for the indivisible salvation of the whole differently from most Kantian theologians. For sociology, nature poses no moral limits to human beings. Nature is there simply to be used, controlled, and reshaped. Moral problems arise only in the human sphere. For ecological theology, as Whitehead said, all 'life is robbery. It is at this point that with life morals become acute. The robber requires justification'.[14] All life involves the taking of food, and in the taking of food animals break down living things into their inorganic elements. Eating involves killing, even when the food is vegetable matter. The killing is more obvious and morally important when we eat the flesh of other animals.

Much more serious is the destruction of habitat by deforestation and expansion of farming. There is also the poisoning of the environment by insecticides and wastes. Our agricultural methods since neolithic times have rendered barren half of the then arable land on the earth. The speed of desertification has been greatly accelerated in our century. All life involves robbery, but modern social life is grand larceny.

Ecology does not teach us that life is unjustified in its robbery. From the fact that something of value is destroyed when we kill an animal, it does not follow that we should stop eating meat, although that is a serious ethical issue. But it does follow that the development of a civilisation which decimates other species casually and threatens to deforest much of the rest of the planet in the next two decades is beyond justification. We have passed all moral limits. An ecological theologian calls for the acceptance of limits to our robbery on moral grounds. We may take what we need. We should not seek to generate and then to satisfy infinite greed.

This conception of moral limits is prior to and independent of the question whether there are actual physical limits. The latter is a matter of fact on which judgements differ. Some believe that with nuclear fusion unlimited sources of energy will be ours and that we can chemically alter the earth's matter so as to replace exhausted resources with others. They believe that ultimately we do not require for our human existence a context of living things. Synthetic food can be produced that will meet all our nutritional needs. A completely artificial environment can be made to simulate any feature of the formerly living world which we require.

Who can say whether all this is possible? An ecological theologian is so revolted morally by this prospect of wholesale destruction of other living things that the question of possibility seems almost irrelevant. Yet there is also scepticism about the possibility. Even if technology could enable us to increase our production and consumption infinitely, are we capable of the perfect social order generation after generation required to protect the nuclear plants and chemical factories from accident or sabotage? Can we abolish war, including wars of liberation? Can we cope with the enormous changes in weather that will result or learn to control them also? Can we replace the ozone layer when it is gone or move underground to escape the deadly rays of the sun? Or can we abandon this planet altogether and find another to destroy? But even if all that is possible, is it not a nightmare? Would it not be better to live morally now, acknowledging limits, than to project such a future for our descendents?

These choices are not distant ones. Continuing commitment to industrial growth in both capitalist and socialist countries is pushing us toward a situation where the nightmare I have pictured could become the only possibility of survival. But it is not too late for a moral choice. We do not *have* to destroy the remaining forests of Amazonia and South-East Asia. We do not *have* to destroy the remainder of the ozone layer. We do not *have* to commit ourselves to an energy policy that will either increase the carbon-dioxide content in the air to the point of making major climatic changes or scatter plutonium around the world. We do not *have* to support Western-type industrialisation as the one path to the good life throughout the tropical world. We do not *have* to continue agricultural practices which are rapidly expanding the world's deserts at the expense of range and farmland. There are moral and practical alternatives. But they require commitment and imagination. Unfortunately those who insist that history is the all-inclusive horizon have been of little help. These ecological concerns fall outside their purview and they lack the sense of moral limits in relation to the rest of nature apart from which sensitivity to these problems rarely arises.

The polemic of this chapter has been against the continuing

influence of Kant in directing attention away from the autonomous existence and inherent importance of the nonhuman world and in supporting a philosophical situation in which human history is the encompassing horizon for thought. Metz systematically adopted and vigorously affirmed these features of the Kantian tradition. Hence the argument has been directed in part toward political theology as he has understood it. There is little in his published writings to indicate that the argument is misdirected. Nevertheless, he is not totally committed to the features of this tradition which have been attacked.

In the first place, his interest in history as the history of suffering and his commitment to solidarity with the oppressed have always run counter to the ignoring of peasants[15] and women and the concentration of attention upon urban—industrial development which have characterised most of those who share his focus upon 'history'. If his published writings to date have not lifted up these concerns, this no doubt reflects the attention of the general culture and the churches rather than the specific consequences of his own theology. The view that history is the encompassing horizon can be combined with a view of human existence which does not centre in the city or even civilisation. But this must be established against meanings of 'political' which have been influential for Metz as well.

In the second place, his 1979 address referred to above runs counter to his earlier writings at a very important point. Earlier he had sharply contrasted the relation to nature and the relation to human beings. He had thought of nature as the world of things, present at hand, which stand at our disposal. He taught that creation and incarnation both declare 'the thing-character of the creature and its general purpose of service to man'.[16] 'Everything in the world is more and more subject to total domination by him and appears as derived directly from him ... This is all fundamentally a Christian event.'[17] Such language, quite appropriate to Metz's Kantian commitments, gave explicit approval to that attitude of domination toward nature which he now opposes as evil. From the point of view of process theology this change is a great gain, but it remains to be seen how fully it can be worked out without deeper alteration in the Kantian philosophy which thus far has shaped his thought.

It may be, indeed, that the change has not gone very far. All along he was aware that there was a danger that attitudes appropriate to nature could too easily be directed toward human beings as well. Even in the recent address it is the dominating attitude toward other human beings that is the primary problem. One could suspect that the only real reason for objecting to the domination of nature is that it leads to the domination of human beings as well. The speed with which he turns from the ecological problem to the social one arouses this suspicion. He associates an interest in an independent nature with Fascism. He states, consistently with his Kantian commitments, that 'nature itself cannot become the principle of a new way of action without some kind of mediation, without some permeation of nature through society and anthropology'.[18] This allows him to keep his concerns fully within the political arena, narrowly understood. Still, the new sensitivity is important, and, from the point of view of process theology, profoundly encouraging.

III

Political theology, in Metz's form, is based on Kantian anthropocentrism. In that context there can be no interest in plants and animals except as they are given being in human experience. Their own interconnectedness and welfare can not constitute a topic of human attention or concern. The model for thinking of the non-human world is taken from stones and machines, and living things are hardly mentioned. Human society and history are the encompassing horizon of reality. Theology which aims to be truly inclusive will be socio-historical theology. It will be more convenient to call it 'sociological theology'.[19]

Process theology, on the other hand, as a development in and from the Chicago school, has been deeply informed by the quite different philosophy of Whitehead. Here humanity is seen within an interconnected nature, all of which is made up of prehensive unifications or occasions of experience. With the appearance of humanity whole new dimensions of reality came into being, but reality itself does not depend on human existence. Theology which aims to be truly inclusive will be 'ecological theology'.

There is no doubt that the term *political theology*, because of its rootage in 'polis', favours attention to human society as the horizon of its concern. Indeed, within the totality of human society, it favours attention to the city. It is in the city that civilisation and history are made. Metz struggles against this further narrowing of attention; for he is interested in the history of the defeated, the powerless, the sufferers. But he is borne along, in part at least, by the overwhelming tendency of those who think within the socio-historical horizon to concentrate upon the city and industrialised civilisation.

Process theology as an ecological theology is concerned about the whole course of nature. Humanity appears as rooted in that nature but also as highly destructive of it. Indeed, humanity is so destructive of its own environment that it threatens to destroy the conditions of its own survival. The problem of food is central. Agriculture is of more basic importance than industry, the peasant village than the city. The human species could survive without the city, and indeed a less urban and less industrial society would have a more promising relationship to the rest of nature. Of course, ecological theology knows that there are cities and that the life of cities is important. Most of its practioners are city-dwellers. There is nothing about the adoption of an ecological perspective that excludes attention to the social structures of urban civilisation. But the tendency of ecological theology is to protest against the dominant preoccupation of sociology and sociological theology with the city and its history and the accompanying neglect of the much larger rural population.

Even if the philosophical differences are not overcome, sociological theology and ecological theology need one another. Sociological theology needs ecological theology in order to widen its horizons to the actual situation of the majority of the human population who face an increasingly desperate and neglected plight in their rural villages. It needs to give much more than passing attention to the decay of the human environment and how this affects the lives and prospects of all human beings. It must recognise that changing the structures of human society and the attitudes of human beings to other human beings in itself is unlikely to solve the environmental problem. Ecological theology needs sociological theology because left to itself it does not deal realistically with the actual structures of power whose exercise will determine human destiny. It does not attend sufficiently to the way economic interests shape convictions and attitudes, including those of

ecological theologians. Further, in its preoccupation with the problem of sustainability of human life and respect for other creatures,
it can too easily lose sight of the enormous suffering and oppression
which can and do take place even in relatively sustainable societies.
Because of its tendency to see what is happening now in a tem-
porally extended context, it needs sociological theology to remind it
of the immediate importance of the present suffering of a single
child. The interaction of sociological theology and ecological theology can lead to an ecologically sensitive sociological theology and
a sociologically sensitive ecological theology.

Whitehead himself did not neglect sociology altogether. He
rightly entitles the first part of *Adventures of Ideas* 'sociological',
and there he shows what it would mean for sociology to be ecologically sensitive. A passage quoted near the end of the preceding
chapter summarised a part of this discussion with an emphasis on
the relation of persuasion to necessity. One of the 'four factors
which decisively govern the fate of social groups' according to his
analysis, is 'the iron compulsion of nature that the bodily necessities of food, clothing and shelter be provided'.[20] Whitehead continues: 'The rigid limits which are thereby set to modes of social
existence can only be mitigated by the growth of an understanding
by which the interplay between man and the rest of nature can be
adjusted.'[21]

Thus, within a strictly sociological analysis, one concerned only
with the human condition and the human future, the interplay between human beings and the rest of nature has its proper place.[22]
That this is so, and, especially, *how* this is so, may be clearer from
the ecological perspective than from the sociological, but it remains
a true and important point about human society, which sociological
theology need not and should not continue to neglect. Whitehead
discussed this feature of sociology repeatedly, especially as he wrestled with the truth, and the limits to truth, of the Malthusian principle. There is much that he wrote on this topic that speaks with un-
diminished relevance today. But he wrote before the human capacity
for total self-destruction had become apparent. He thought in terms
of a multiplicity of civilisations and of how the Malthusian principle
was rendered inoperative in some over long periods of time. Today
we must consider the relevance of Malthus on a global scale, and
such considerations should be a part of our sociology.

The problems of freedom and equality, and therefore of justice, were at the centre of Whitehead's sociological concerns, and they have been important for all process theology. An ecological theology is not indifferent to justice. Sociological theology has focused on questions of justice, but as it has recognised that the effects of human beings on their environment are having seriously deleterious consequences for humanity, it has extended its concern to questions of the sustainability of human society.[23] Yet in practice the difference of the amount of attention given to these two issues of justice and sustainability still leads to opposing judgements on important issues.

These issues are too often dealt with in the context of the trade-off mentality described in the preceding chapter. It is thought that the requirements of justice and of sustainability are in tension with one another, and those who are preoccupied with justice are reluctant to make concessions to the needs of sustainability. They are still at times inclined to regard the latter concerns as a luxury only the comfortable can afford. As long as justice and sustainability are viewed as antagonistic interests, sociological theology and ecological theology will work against each other, whereas they are both needed in a truly comprehensive political theology. They can work together only when, abandoning the trade-off mentality, the adherents of both rethink the requirements of both justice and sustainability so as to see that justice entails sustainability and sustainability entails justice.

This is not difficult to do. As Metz has seen, attitudes toward the natural environment and toward other people deeply influence each other. He has not yet shown awareness of the full meaning of this especially as women have shown us how it has affected male attitudes toward them. But in principle the general point is now widely recognised. We are unlikely to put an end to the exploitation of human beings unless we also bring an end to the exploitative attitude toward the natural environment.

In additon, justice cannot mean only justice to those who are now living. It must include justice to generations yet unborn. That demands a sustainable relationship to the environment. On the other side, a society many of whose members find themselves oppressed is inherently unstable, and without social stability there can be no ecological sustainability either. To enforce, in the name of ecological sustainability, policies that violate the sense of justice of the people involved introduces an element that is very likely to make those policies unsustainable.[24]

The mutual support of justice and sustainability has more concrete meaning as well. It means that, for the most part, the policies that are now operating to destroy the capacity of the environment to support human life in the future are also expressions of the injustice of present distribution of wealth and power. On the whole, remedies proposed to attain justice will, or can, support sustainability as well, and vice versa.

For example, there is a high correlation between the concentration of land ownership in a few hands and the degradation of the soil. In some countries, as in the United States, this is connected with agribusiness' viewing the soil as a capital investment to be depreciated as it is used up, whereas the family farmer typically wishes to pass the farm on to children in good condition. In Third World countries it is related to the fact that the best land is often owned by a few families or corporations and used for the production of crops for export. Subsistence farmers are then forced to till land that is not suitable for agriculture. As a result of this all too typical pattern of unjust land distribution, for example, 77 percent of the land in El Salvador, where fourteen families control the wealth, is suffering from erosion, according to a recent study.[25] A more just distribution of land would greatly reduce the negative impact on the environment.

This is not an isolated case. The preceding chapter noted that Amory Lovins has developed in detail a proposal for soft energy paths which is at once environmentally beneficial and encouraging of a wider distribution of more satisfactory employment, of power, and of wealth. Other studies are increasingly supporting his view that more efficient use of the energy now produced can meet all real needs and that the United States can shift from vast centralised systems of energy production to others which are accessible to regional and local control.

Efficient use of energy for transportation also tends in the direction of justice. Thus far, many development programmes in Third World countries have taxed the poor in order that the few who can own private motorcars may ride in comfort. These same private cars are the most wasteful form of transportation from the point of view of exhausting scarce resources. A transportation system that emphasises the widespread availability of the bicycle supplemented by trucks and buses and trains is both preferable from the environmental point of view and more equitable.

The way cities have developed in much of the world is such that they remove much prime agricultural land from cultivation and can function only through vast consumption of energy and other scarce resources. At the same time they are such that the poor are excluded from public advantages and segregated into those parts of the city that are least well-served. The city dweller who is without wealth is unable to escape the urban environment so as to enjoy a natural one. Massive alienation is the inevitable result, with the accompanying increase of crimes. Paolo Soleri has conceived of an alternative form of urban life in which the architectural ecology — arcology for short — would promote both justice and the environment. His beautiful structures would soar into the air, releasing most of the land now covered by urban sprawl for agriculture, recreation, or wilderness. Within the arcology distances would be such that elevators, escalators and moving sidewalks would combine with walking to make all the city's facilities available to all. Similarly everyone would be able to walk outside of the city into its rural environment. Such cities could operate on a small fraction of the energy consumed by our present cities and they could be so built that most of the requisite energy could be provided directly by the sun.

In these and many other ways the supposition that policies guided by justice should conflict with those guided by sustainability can be shown to be factually and dangerously wrong. Our God-given imagination can provide us with a vision of a possible future that is both much more just and much more sustainable than our present world. The trade-off is not the helpful image for moving us toward this new world.

This point can be illustrated in another way as well. It is rightly stressed that no sustainable society is possible apart from population stability.[26] Such stability cannot be attained at once, but there is great importance in developing policies which will rapidly slow population growth around the world and bring it to a halt at no more than six billion. Unfortunately, when there is talk of reducing population growth by public policies, many people immediately envision serious infringements on the freedom of families to make decisions about the number of children they shall have. Civil libertarians rise to the defence of this private freedom while those concerned for the global good seem prepared to adopt penalties that severely limit personal freedom.

Of course such tensions are inevitable. But the supposition that the only way to limit population growth is to restrict personal freedom is a major obstacle to creative action today. The supposition is false. The major way to slow population growth is to increase personal freedom, especially for women. Study after study has shown that when women have real freedom to choose they opt for fewer children. In those countries in which women not only have a great deal of freedom to control their own bodies but also are free to share in public life on a nearly equal basis with men, the birth rates have already fallen to equal the death rates. Indeed, some governments are fearful of a loss of population! The problems are complex. But the emancipation of women for the sake of justice is the key to the stabilisation of global population.

In the case of the emancipation of women and the birth rate it should be recognised that the reduced birth rate is largely an unforeseen and unintended result of social change. Here it seems that pursuit of justice alone would suffice and that the other problem would take care of itself. This is an exaggeration even in this instance. Governments concerned to slow their birth rates will support the freedom of women to limit the number of their children more than will governments which are insensitive to this need. What is important is to keep in view the simultaneous need to free women and to reduce the birth rate and to encourage policies that achieve both.

In other areas the direct quest for immediate justice is not likely to generate the requisite policies, for reasons suggested earlier in this chapter. For example, just as those preoccupied with 'justice' have paid little attention to the subsistence farmer, so also they have paid little attention to the world's most urgent energy crisis — the shortage of firewood. It is those who focus on the environment who have long been calling attention to the manifold negative consequences of deforestation and have concerned themselves with how this situation could be reversed.

The shortage of firewood is not a function of obvious injustices in ownership and distribution. It is a function of the pressure of growing population on the environment, combined with neglect of the problems of that segment of the population most dependent on firewood. I refer to the peasantry. Governments in most Third World countries, supported by development policies in First and Second World countries, have been concerned about supplying sophisticated forms of energy for industrialisation and urban life. They have been too little concerned with the simple technological changes needed for more efficient use of firewood as a fuel for cooking. Nor have they helped villagers to develop woodlots near at hand which would meet their needs and reduce the pressure on the increasingly distant wooded mountainsides. The beginning of a shift of attention to these matters has come about because persons concerned for the preservation of forests have also been concerned that ordinary people should be able to cook their food. Sustainability and justice here, too, belong together, but without ecological sensitivities neither is attained.

The concerns I have been pressing are not in principle excluded from sociological theology. They fall within history. But since the interest here is practical, it is important to recognise that in fact those who have turned for guidance to sociology have rarely been helpful in directing attention to many of these types of problems and solutions. The lead has been taken in most instances by those who have a lively interest in the environment. This should say something to those who are committed to the praxis model!

If there emerges a sociology which is truly sensitive to ecological issues, and if ecological theology truly assimilates the insights that can be learned only from sociology, that will be a great gain. The gap between such a new sociological theology and a new ecological one will be narrowed. But it will not be erased.

Ecological theology will not limit its concern for the environment to its role in the sustaining of human societies. From the point of view of process theologians, justice requires that the rest of the creation should also be treated with respect and recognised to have reality and value quite apart from usefulness to human beings. Other creatures are of value in themselves and for God. Unless it breaks fundamentally from the Kantian tradition, even an ecologically sensitive sociological theology can not acknowledge this inherent reality and worth of our fellow creatures. But not to do so, for ecological theology, is profoundly false to the Biblical vision.[27]

It would be unfortunate if at this point the trade-off model once again controlled thought and action. There may be times when human beings should make real sacrifices so that other species can continue to exist, even when these species are of no value to humanity. But for the most part what is truly good for human beings and what is truly good for other species will coincide when problems are faced with good will and imagination. The preservation of the tropical forests is essential if we are not to decimate the planet's wildlife. It is also essential if we are not to alter the human environment in ways that could be disastrous for the next generation. Concern for the least and most powerless of our fellow creatures may at times save us from suicidal action! But ecological theology will insist that our concern for these creatures must not be motivated only by our desire for human welfare. It is this important element which a Kantian theology does not include.

NOTES

1   It is disappointing that sensitivity to the natural environment is not expressed in such later writings of Sölle as *Beyond Mere Dialogue: On Being Christian and Socialist* (Detroit, Mich.: American Christians Toward Socialism, 1978).

2   Jürgen Moltmann, *The Crucified God*, trans. R. A. Wilson and John Bowden (New York: Harper & Row, 1974), p. 334. See also Moltmann, *Experiences of God*, trans. Margaret Kohl (Philadelphia, Pa: Fortress Press, 1980), p. 27.

3   Johann Baptist Metz, *Faith in History and Society: Toward a Practical Fundamental Theology*, trans. David Smith (New York: Seabury Press, 1980), pp. 106–7.

4   Johann Baptist Metz, *Christliche Anthropozentrik: Über die Denkform des Thomas von Aquin* (Munich: Kosel Verlag, 1962), p. 68. (My translation.)

5   *Ibid.*, p. 69. (My translation.)

6   *Ibid.* (My translation.)

7   Roger Dick Johns, *Man in the World: the Political Theology of Johannes Baptist Metz* (Missoula, Mont.: Scholars Press, 1976), p. 87.

8   *Ibid.*, p. 89.

9   Johann Baptist Metz, 'Mitsein', in *Lexikon für Theologie und Kirche* vol. 7, cols. 492–3. The English translation is from Johns, pp. 97–8.

10 See Paul R. Ehrlich and Anne H. Ehrlich, *Extinction: the Causes and Consequences of the Disappearance of Species* (New York: Random House, 1981).

11 Robert Heilbroner, *An Inquiry into the Human Prospect* (New York: Norton, 1974).

12 Johann Baptist Metz, 'Bread of Survival: The Lord's Supper of Christians as Anticipatory Sign of an Anthropological Revolution', in *The Emergent Church*, trans. Peter Mann (New York: Crossroad, 1981), p. 41. On page 34 Mann translates 'sog. Überlebenskrise' as 'what is called our crisis of survival'. This removes the pejorative force which I have retained in my translation as 'so-called crisis of survival'.

13 Irene Tinker, Michelin Bo Bramsen and Mayra Buvinič, eds., 'The adverse impact of development on women', in *Women in World Development* (New York: Praeger Publishers, 1976), p. 23.

14 Alfred North Whitehead, *Process and Reality*, corrected ed. by David Ray Griffin and Donald W. Sherburne (New York: The Free Press, 1978), p. 105.

15 See Metz, *Faith in History and Society*, p. 66.

16 Johann Baptist Metz, 'Unbelief as a theological problem', trans. Tarcisius Rattler in *The Church and the World*, Concilium, vol. 6 (New York: Paulist Press, 1965), p. 76.

17 Johann Baptist Metz, *Theology of the World*, trans. William Glen-Doepel (New York: Herder & Herder, 1971), p. 38.

18 Metz, 'Bread of Survival', pp. 34—5.

19 This term was applied to Metz by Erik Rupp, 'Der Deutsche Emanzipations-katholizismus 1968/69', in *Kritischer Katholizismus*, ed. Ben van Onna and Martin Stankowski (Frankfurt: Fischer Bücherei, 1969), pp. 49—56. The context and meaning are different from mine.

20 Alfred North Whitehead, *Adventures of Ideas* (New York: The Free Press, 1933), p. 108.

21 *Ibid.*, pp. 108—9.

22 It is significant that the September/October 1980 issue of *American Behavioral Scientist* is devoted to 'Ecology and the social sciences: an emerging paradigm'. The lead essay begins with the statement: 'The social sciences have largely ignored the fact that human societies depend on the biophysical environment for their survival.' Riley E. Dunlap, 'Paradigmatic change in social science: from human exemptions to an ecological paradigm', p. 5.

23 The Church and Society sub-unit of the World Council of Churches deserves special credit for having brought its sociologically oriented constituency to this recognition ratified in 1979 at the MIT Conference. See Paul Abrecht, ed., *Faith and Science in an Unjust World: Report of the World Council of Churches Conference on Faith, Science and The Future* (Geneva: World Council of Churches, 1980).

24 Mrs Gandhi's earlier political defeat was connected to her birth control policies.

25 Howard Edward Daugherty, *Man Induced Ecological Change in El Salvador*. PhD. dissertation, University of California, Berkeley, Dept. of Geography, 1969. Reference is made by Erik P. Eckholm, *Losing Ground* (New York: W. W. Norton, 1976), pp. 168—9.

26 The best available short statement on population is Lester R. Brown, *Resource Trends and Population Policy: a Time for Reassessment* (Washington, D.C.: Worldwatch Institute, 1979).

27 See George S. Hendry, *Theology of Nature* (Philadelphia, Pa.: Westminster Press, 1980).

Chapter Seven

A THEOLOGY
OF HISTORY

In the preceding chapter the argument with Metz was about features of his thought that are governed by his philosophical commitment to the Kantian tradition. This necessitates the radical anthropocentricity which he affirms and embodies in his political theology. It is proposed that a Whiteheadian ecological theology is today more appropriate to the indivisible salvation of the whole world. Such a theology strains the meaning of 'political', but it can and should conform to all those features originally proposed in the characterisation of political theology by Metz, Moltmann and Sölle, and it carries forward its essential spirit.

In this chapter the features of Metz that are treated are more properly theological. They do not follow from his Kantian anthropocentricity but from his Christian Christocentricity. They are attractive and appealing to a process theologian in their positive meaning. But Metz so develops them as to exclude theological interest in an overview of history. From the perspective of process thought, too, a theology of history has dangers, but there are strong Christian reasons for developing one.

Section I explains Metz's position and its existentially powerful outcome, but it also considers the limits which this position places upon Christian thinking and practice. Section II summarises the Whiteheadian theology of history as an example of the kind of overview that is needed to guide practice in many areas. Section III reflects on the limitations of that kind of practice which is directed by such an overview. Section IV concludes the chapter and the book by reaffirming the central intention that process theology must become a political theology.

I

Metz is quite clear that his project of a practical fundamental theology is a radical development in theology. It is correlated with the conviction that there are just two possibilities for theology, and that the alternative possibility, the one followed by almost everyone, is disastrous. This alternative is to accept the overwhelmingly prevalent view which he calls evolutionary and to explain Christianity and Christian beliefs within that context.

By 'evolutionary' Metz does not have in mind the specific theory employed in biology. Nor does he refer especially to those thinkers who have explicitly extrapolated from biology. His meaning is closer to what others might call historical; for he is thinking of any effort to understand human occurrences in terms of how they can be located and explained in the wider course of events.

It is not only scholars and theologians who are prone to evolutionary thinking. This mode of consciousness is 'present as a kind of feeling for life, in man's pre-scientific consciousness and has as such impressed itself on modern man's everyday experience of life'.[1] As a result 'man's consciousness of his own identity has become weaker and more damaged in the course of human progress. Man is at the mercy of a darkly speckled universe and enclosed in an endless continuum of time that is no longer capable of surprising him. He feels that he is caught up in the waves of an anonymous process of evolution sweeping pitilessly over everyone'.[2] Metz fears that 'the feeling of being locked into an infinite, empty, anonymous time — called "evolution" — has long since extinguished any substantial sense of hope or expectation'.[3] But he believes that prayer functions as resistance to this apathy.

When theologians adopt the evolutionary point of view, Metz thinks, their work can be 'regarded, with different degrees of explicitness, as meta-theories with respect to religion and theology. In other words, religion can, for the purpose of these theories, in principle be either reconstructed or abolished and seen as pointing to a more comprehensive theoretical system'.[4] By locating religion in a larger explanatory context it gives 'its public claim to validity a purely relative value'.[5]

Metz is convinced that faith cannot accept this relativisation, and accordingly it is 'an essential task of fundamental theology ... to defend, justify or give an account of the authenticity of religion, in opposition to those systems that claim to be meta-theories of theology'.[6] It cannot do this by developing a still more comprehensive overview. It can only 'justify itself as theology by a return to subjects and the praxis of subjects'.[7]

Metz is responding to the same problem faced by Barth. Liberal theology gave an account of Christianity as one phenomenon alongside others, explaining its particular value and importance. It might claim that religion is of supreme importance for everyone and that Christianity is the absolute religion. But even in making such claims it presented Christianity as a relative phenomenon which required justification in terms of more objective norms than its own claims and self-understanding. Barth rejected this liberal approach. Nevertheless in many guises it has returned. As Metz notes, almost everyone understands the various religious movements as just that, phenomena which differ from each other and require an explanation and justification in terms of criteria that are not their own. The sheer affirmation of one or another faith by those unwilling to submit their assertions to testing in a more neutral court is dismissed as fideism. Yet to understand one's own faith as one among many and in need of justification beyond itself relativises that faith in one's own eyes. The only real absolute is the court of appeal in which justification is required. Metz refers to this as a meta-theory. But of course there are many meta-theories. The result is a loss of confidence.

Metz is convinced theology cannot accept this relativisation of faith, but it cannot establish itself by fideistic claims. That means that fundamental theology can no longer be theoretical. He believes it can be practical. Its affirmations will be authentic to the extent that they represent real practice. That practice will appeal to vindication in the future, for Metz, the apocalyptic future.

Metz knows that the power of the evolutionary consciousness is not easily broken and that it can absorb his practical, fundamental theology as well. Hence he not only polemicises against its mode of thinking but also points out that it is itself a socio-historical product. The world constituted for us by this mode of experience 'is in fact a secondary meta-world, in other words, a world which, in itself and in its deepest reality, bears the deep impression of many systems and theories and which can therefore only be experienced and possibly changed in and through these systems and theories'.[8] It is clear that

Metz would like to overcome this evolutionary world and replace it, at least for Christians, by the apocalyptic one. But he does not underestimate the difficulty. Meanwhile he calls for a Christian practice and reflection in the midst of that practice.

These reflections of Metz need to be taken with utmost seriousness. There is a profound difference between thinking about faith from a perspective that is informed by an overview of history and thinking in and from the faith itself. Metz is correct that the latter is possible for us today only when the faith from which we think is the practice of faith, a practice which seeks its vindication in the fulfilment it expects rather than in victory over competing beliefs in the court of some supposedly neutral overview. Since faith does not arise through rational conviction of a superior conceptual system, but instead through the memory of past events and especially the passion of Jesus, its embodiment in practice does not depend on any overview — only on the effective power of the memory.

Metz shows in this way how Christian practice gains its distinctive character. It is not dependent on determining what is most appropriate from a general ethical system. The memory of suffering and of God's calling people to themselves as subjects leads directly to participating in the suffering of the world and trying to help all people become the subjects they truly are. It recovers, therefore, the uncalculating element in Christian practice. It sets aside many of the problems of practicality which so often inhibit us. It enables the suffering love remembered in Jesus's passion to be actualised again.

Metz contrasts this with what is actually occurring in the church:

> There is an increasing loss of deep inner conviction regarding faith in the official Church today, resulting in a corresponding loss of nerve and decisiveness. The life of the Church is characterized by a fear of powers and processes that are not understood. This anxiety has sapped the courage of Christians to take new steps, encourage the development of new, alternative forms of Christian praxis and to make new religious and political experiments. This anxiety has led to a quest for stabilization in past forms.[8]

Attractive as Metz's proposal of how to counter this decay of faith is, it cannot be adopted by process theology without extensive modifications, modifications so great that its particular values may be lost. For process theology the quest for the overview within which to understand particular phenomena, including Christian faith, cannot be given up. It is significant that Metz's book provides such an overview as justification for rejecting the overview approach. He himself knows how deeply this necessity is rooted in our consciousness, and how difficult it would be to free ourselves from it. It is by his particular overview that he concluded that secularisation is the product of creation and incarnation. This is not an argument against his proposal; for there are no easy answers in the modern world. The question is whether faith requires us to oppose the quest for the overview. Process theology thinks it does not, that the price, specifically from the point of view of faith, would be too high. It seems to involve a narrowing which in process perspective is antithetical to faith. This was discussed in Chapter Three as it bears on the relation of faith to other religious traditions.

More generally Metz's programme seems to abandon the Biblical mode of historical consciousness. Without an overview people cannot locate themselves in the course of history and thus understand what is appropriate for their time and place. The structure of the Bible itself presents such an overview. And I have suggested that Metz's own writings present another.

But these criticisms in part misrepresent Metz's more nuanced position. He writes: 'My criticism, then, is principally directed against the attempt to explain the historical identity of Christianity by means of speculative thought (idealism), without regard to the constitutive function of Christian praxis, the cognitive equivalent of which is narrative and memory.'[10] Elsewhere he identifies the evolutionary thought which he opposes as 'a basic acceptance of technical rationality'.[11] He speaks of Wolfhart Pannenberg's 'extremely valuable attempt to develop a universally historical hermeneutics', complaining only that his 'anticipation of a total meaning in history is ... too little interrupted or irritated by what is described in the apocalyptic tradition as a universal catastrophe, in other words, the reign of the Antichrist'.[12] Metz is more open to an overview than some of his statements imply.

The difference might be that any pretence that an overview is objective or neutral is to be abandoned. If so, a process theologian can agree. There is no point from which to gain an overview other than the socio-culturally influenced locus where one is. Although human beings are free to transcend the determinism of that locus in both thought and action, especially by examining it and seeing how it affects them, they cannot think from a neutral or objective point outside of their concrete history. Overviews may be more and less ideological, more and less relevant to persons with highly diverse perspectives, but they always bear the marks of their situation.

Having abandoned the pretense of neutrality one might propose that Christian theology should be or include a Christian overview. Certainly it has played that role in the past, and Metz's appreciation of Pannenberg suggests that he does not exclude this. But Metz does deny that fundamental theology can justify itself by 'developing another and even more comprehensive theory which might be a theological meta-theory of the existing world theories'.[13]

Regardless of how Metz ultimately resolves this question, process theology must seek the solution in a different direction. It cannot oppose the relativisation of every content of Christian faith, even the events of suffering which it remembers. It is open to all the meta-theories through which the content of faith is relativised, while rejecting their attempts to avoid their own relativisation. It judges everything historical, without exception, to be relative. It supports the critical spirit without limit. It sees this spirit at work in the effort to gain an overview which relativises every particular and also in the criticism of the overview both from the perspective of the particular and by more adequate and inclusive overviews. It perceives faith in the recognition of the relativity of all things human, including one's own self, and in openness to transformation. That which transforms, it understands as God incarnate in the world as Christ. That incarnation is seen everywhere because it is seen first and decisively in Jesus's life, message, passion and resurrection. Faith is the memory of all of the ways in which God has acted to relativise the world and transform it — a memory which is illumined throughout by the narrative of Jesus, which warns us against establishing even our relation to that narrative as absolute and which opens us to transformation in the present by the new that now comes.[14]

With this understanding and experience of faith, process theologians can share in the criticism of every objectifying and deterministic overview and of every failure to appreciate the decisive transforming work of Christ. But the quest for new and better overviews, overviews more fully informed by the memory of the passion of Jesus and the recognition of the universal working of Christ, is itself the work of Christ. The overviews are created goods, not to be clung to, but to be used and, in their turn, relativised.

If a fundamental theology is a solid and unchangeable ground on which to build, then from the point of view of process theology, there can be no fundamental theology, not even a practical one. There is no such ground. Every 'fundamental theology' is at best another created good which Christ as the creative good will relativise and supersede. It is the acceptance of that situation, rather than its overcoming, for which faith calls in the view of process theology.

An overview which relativises the Christian religion and even the relation to the passion of Jesus is not then to be opposed on principle. Indeed, it is to be sought, especially when the absolutisation of the relation to Jesus threatens to close us to other relations. But an overview is important in other ways. Since political practice is our special concern, let us consider it here.

Metz knows that we cannot move mindlessly from the memory of the passion of Jesus to responsible political action in our world. We require as much understanding as possible of our present political situation. For this we can certainly turn to the social sciences. But there are two limitations of this approach.

First, when we turn to the social sciences we do not find neutral objective disciplines which can provide the tools and information we need. We find instead bodies of thought impregnated by assumptions and points of view which should themselves be relativised and reconstructed from the perspective of contemporary Christian faith. We need the help of social sciences in which the process of such relativisation and reconstruction is somewhat advanced. But we cannot go far in this direction without a Christian overview.

Second, the combination of sociological analysis with solidarity with those who suffer does not suffice to guide us in many of the concrete political problems of today's world. Israel is one example. If we look sociologically at the state of Israel today we will find there quite typical examples of the oppression and suffering of a powerless minority, in this case the Arabs.

One Christian response would be to attempt to achieve some reconciliation between Arab interests and Jewish interests through complex negotiations. It may well be that Metz personally favours such efforts. But here we are concerned not with his actual judgements but with the implications of what he has written as a theologian. He writes that the church must have and act upon 'an unconditional commitment to justice, freedom and peace *for others*'.[15]

> If, indeed, we may not immediately and directly agree on the positive meaning of freedom, peace and justice, we all share a long-standing and common experience of what these things are *not*. And so this negative experience offers us an opportunity to unite, less, perhaps, in the positive planning of the freedom and justice we are seeking than in our critical opposition to the horror and terror of unfreedom and injustice. The solidarity bred by this experience, the possibility, therefore, of a common front of protest, must be understood and put into action.[16]

If we act directly on this call, combined with an analysis of the structure of power in Israel today, we will seek justice for the Arabs regardless of the threat to the future of a Jewish state. Before we do that we need to remember many other things, especially the way the passion of Jesus has been employed through millenia by Christian believers for the oppression of Jews.[17] We should consider also the need of a people for a homeland, an issue poorly illumined by either the memory of the passion of Jesus alone or contemporary social sciences. Indeed, we can only formulate political policies in relation to Israel in the context of an inclusive overview of human history. In seeking such an overview we must avoid the pitfalls Metz notes: the pretence of neutrality, the positivistic tendency, the forgetting of the subject and the denial of the openness of the future. But we can avoid these negative features of evolutionary thought better by offering an improved picture than by attempting to eradicate the need for any picture at all.

II

Concrete judgements responsibly directive of political practice cannot derive from the memory of Jesus's passion even when one is informed by the social sciences. The meaning of what is occurring in the world can be derived only from an overview of what has happened in the past and its significance for the present. From Augustine to Hegel and Marx such overviews played a crucial role in shaping Western thought and specifically Christian theology. But in recent times they have fallen into disrepute.

One problem has been that they have been seen as *philosophies* of history, and philosophy has been expected to avoid the pitfalls of speculation. It has tried to define itself in such a way that it can achieve certainty. This has driven it to abandon the larger fields of synthetic thought and to accept logic, the analysis of language, and phenomenological description as its special province. Philosophy of history in the older sense is thereby excluded. Yet people cannot but operate with some conscious or unconscious view of where we now are in relation to where we have been in the past, and an occasional historian and psychiatrist has stepped in to fill the void left by philosophers and theologians. The resulting interpretations are rarely acceptable from the point of view of the Christian. Metz's protests are in this respect well taken. But if we cannot engage in responsible political practice without an historically informed view of what is taking place, and if the views offered us by others are not satisfactory, then Christians, for the sake of political practice, should enter the field, recognising that they do so from their own perspective, shaped by the memory of Jesus. What we then would develop would be a theology of history.

There does not exist at present a theology of history that is anywhere close to adequate to our needs. If such a theology of history existed, it could do much to remedy the sad state of the church of which Metz wrote so movingly. As Metz calls programmatically for a practical fundamental theology to respond to this problem, I am calling for a theology of history as a partial response.

Bits and pieces of theology of history are to be found in many journals of Christian opinion. They implicitly constitute the stuff of many a conversation about current events. Reinhold Niebuhr made a more sustained contribution in such works as *The Irony of American History*.[18] Teilhard de Chardin offered a different perspective in *The Phenomenon of Man*.[19] Van Leeuwen develops a rich and fruitful approach in *Christianity in World History*.[20]

The theologian who has done most to awaken us to the need for a theology of history is Wolfhart Pannenberg. He holds that meaningful interpretation of the course of events is possible only by a pre-apprehension of the fulfilling outcome toward which they move. Certainly this has been the dominant pattern of Western philosophy and theology of history through Marx. And without some vision of a future worth hoping for, an overview of history can be no guide to practice. The loss of expectation of a consummatory End of history is no doubt a major reason for the decline both of faith and of reflection about the meaning of history. But from the point of view of process theology, the need now is to renew the Christian interpretation of history without presupposing a fulfilling End. Some of Pannenberg's interpretations, as for example in *Human Nature, Election, and History*,[21] can be appropriated by process theology as valuable contributions to such an open-ended theology of history.

Process theology is clearer in its call for a theology of history than in any proposal it can make to meet this need. Scattered contributions have been made.[22] But the best work in this tradition has been done by Whitehead himself.

Whitehead's theology of history is entitled *Adventures of Ideas.* It was not written as a single book but developed out of several lectures and sets of lectures. Accordingly it might be more properly called the material for a theology of history than the theology itself.

To speak of a theology of history betrays my conclusion that Whitehead is to be considered a Christian thinker despite the fact that he does not clearly identify himself as such. He is a Christian thinker in much the same way that Kant and Hegel are. None of them, as philosophers, merely provide an abstract philosophical conceptuality which theologians are then able to use. The very fact that they are not professionally committed to supporting the faith contributes to the Christian authenticity of what they say. All three were deeply shaped by Christianity in their childhood and youth; all wrestled with Jesus Christ in their philosophical work and attributed a central role to him; all rejected the orthodoxies of their times; all contributed to the refashioning of Christianity. This, I take it, is the proper work of a truly free Christian thinker.

The first requisite to having a theology of history is belief in freedom. If there is no freedom, the enterprise makes no sense. Things simply are what they are, and evaluation and judgement are meaningless. There is no point in interpreting what is occurring, if that interpretation can have no effect upon behaviour.

Preceding chapters have outlined features of Whitehead's ontology that are relevant to this question. He sees every occasion of experience as arising out of its world, including that world, and being necessarily constituted by it. At the same time he sees every occasion as finally making a decision as to just how it shall include that world and be constituted by it.

At the human, historical level, the constituting elements include physical necessities, customs, habits, unquestioned opinions and coercion. Most of what happens most of the time can be largely understood as the working of these blind forces. But this is not the whole story. There are also human purposes which stand in tension with the given. Most of these are thwarted. But there are fortunate cases when the material at hand is shaped to the attainment of purpose. Whitehead gives the example of the control of fire, 'which obediently to human purpose cooks and gives warmth. In fact,' he continues, 'freedom of action is a primary human need. In modern thought the expression of this truth has taken the form of "the economic interpretation of history".'[23]

Human purposes are affected by ideas. Such ideas may be assimilated from the cultural matrix uncritically. As such they are part of the determinism of our situation. But ideas can also be abstracted from this matrix as possibilities for acceptance or rejection, and relevant new ideas can arise. In this role these function persuasively, and not coercively. These persuasive ideas, too, can inform purposes and lead to institutional embodiment.

The extent to which we are moved by persuasion rather than by the force of the constituting world is a measure of the extent to which we are free. Of course, there is no such thing as absolute freedom, and Whitehead does not deplore the role of the world in constituting us. Nevertheless, the expansion of freedom is a real gain in terms of which we can measure the advance and decline of history. It provides a principle for interpreting the meaning of historical movements, whether the end of history will be failure or consummation.

The expansion of freedom is both a matter of extending the areas of individual life in which we are free and of expanding the number of people who are free. Hence one main aspect of progress in the modern world has been the abolition of slavery. Whitehead studies this in some detail. He emphasises that technology made possible a society in which the necessary work can be done without slavery. But he also stresses the role of Plato's doctrine of the soul as this was assimilated into Christianity and later into humanism. It took two thousand years to achieve 'the final inversion of sociological theory, from the presupposition of slavery to the presupposition of freedom'.[24]

This illustrates the complex relation between ideas and institutions. Plato did not contemplate a society without slaves despite the critique of slavery implicit in his doctrine. By the time this implication of his idea was realised in *practice*, the doctrine was losing acceptance among intellectuals, who were discussing Malthus and Hume and social Darwinism.

Despite the ironies inherent in this situation, Whitehead does believe that there has been real progress. He prefers the ideas of Plato to those of Malthus, Hume, and social Darwinism, but he prefers the implementation of Plato's ideas to their abstract entertainment. He knows that the aboltion of slavery does not constitute the full meaning of the Platonic—Christian doctrine, but he takes satisfaction in the change that has occurred. 'When all such qualifications have been made,' he writes, 'Freedom and Equality constitute an inevitable presupposition of modern political thought, with an admixture of subsequent lame qualification; while Slavery was a corresponding presupposition for the ancients, with their admixture of lame qualification.'[25]

Implicit in Whitehead's analysis is a statement of his own intended contribution to human freedom and equality. Much of modern thought has abandoned not only the word soul but also any ontological grounding for the worth and dignity of human beings. Those who abolish the idea of the soul do not intend to encourage slavery, any more than Plato understood himself as the emancipator. But modern positivist and physicalist ideas, as they are widely assimilated and reshape the common sense of the West, will have unintended effects. This may not take two thousand years! It is important for an affirmation of the human soul congruent with our best contemporary knowledge to be introduced to challenge these implicitly dehumanising ideas. Whitehead offers us such an anthropology.

For Whitehead freedom and equality belong together because the most important form of equality is the equality of freedom. This does not mean for him abstract freedom. Freedom should include legal rights, but it is certainly not exhausted by them. Freedom is always present in its inevitably limited way in concrete situations which are socially and economically as well as physically conditioned. The removal of barriers to freedom is always appropriate unless it causes greater loss of freedom somewhere else. In his argument for the enfranchisement of women he formulated his principle succinctly:

I base my adherence to the cause upon the old-fashioned formula of liberty: That is upon the belief that in the life of a rational being it is an evil when the circumstances affecting him are beyond his control, and are not amenable to his intelligent direction and comprehension. External constraint upon the rational self-direction of conduct is, indeed, inextricably interwoven in the nature of things. But wherever it exists, and is removable without some corresponding loss of liberty, it is evil, it is the enemy.[26]

III

In a general sense Whitehead is close to Metz in the conclusions which he draws from this anthropology. Metz wants all people fully to realise themselves as free subjects. Whitehead is equally concerned with the realisation of freedom by all. Both are concerned to reduce the coercive factors in life as far as possible. But there are apparent differences as well.

In the first place Whitehead's presentation is not obviously Christocentric. In the brief summary above, Plato appeared as the hero of the story. It would have been possible to summarise Whitehead's views quite differently, showing the very central place he does in fact accord to Jesus in this story.[27] But it is better to let the difference be manifest. Whitehead views the total course of events with commitments which, it is here claimed, are Christian. He sees the great, even central, importance of Jesus, but he is under no compulsion to emphasise this, and he examines carefully the contributions of others, Christians and not, to the realisation of what Christians seek. This form of Christocentricity is completely open to all historical movements and sources.

In the second place Whitehead attributes to the history of thought relative independence in relation to the history of institutions. This involves some modification of the praxis model, although it certainly does not minimise the importance of practice. The interaction of idea and practice is fully dialectical for Whitehead.

But there are other differences between Whitehead and Metz which are more directly relevant for practice. Whitehead's commitment to the increase of freedom does not stress the Christian point that God sides with the oppressed and that we are called to solidarity with them. The general support of freedom and equality lacks the pathos of the Christian affirmation and can too easily be appropriated within a bourgeois framework without breaking that structure. Nevertheless, the difference between Metz and Whitehead is not as great as may at first appear. Metz, on his side, denies that any one party or class should see itself as the subject of universal history;[28] and Whitehead's vision allows, even requires, an argument that supports the Christian concern for 'the least'.

Whitehead calls for us so to act as to maximise the richness of experience of all. To do so is to remove unnecessary external constraints upon the rational self-direction of conduct. These unnecessary constraints do not operate chiefly upon the rich and powerful but upon the poor and oppressed.[29] It is among them that there exists the greatest gap between the quality of experience now realised and what they are capable of realising as circumstances change. Hence the call to maximise the quality of experience generally directs us primarily to changing the conditions that now constrain the oppressed. This would mean making possible sufficient food and other necessities on the basis of a degree and type of labour that is itself enriching rather than debilitating. It would mean also providing those stimuli which are most likely to lead to adventures of thought and feeling. And it would mean empowering those who are now powerless to take charge of their own destinies.

A moral problem arises as to the justification of expending energies for the increase of the freedom of the already privileged. It is often supposed that in general the lot of the poor can be improved only at the expense of the rich. In this case working with and for the rich can only function negatively with respect to the poor. The conclusion would be a severe condemnation of those of us, for example, who make our living as professors in First World universities seeking to help the privileged students who attend them.

Certainly there are many instances when the possessions of the rich must be redistributed if the poor are to gain significant freedom. But if we think of the enhancement of freedom and enrichment of experience as something quite different from the increase or preservation of material wealth — and this difference is clear in the case of the rich, if not in that of the extremely poor — then working for the true benefit of the privileged is in itself positive. Process theology favours images of change in which all grow in freedom and in a correlative richness of experience.

Such statements, however, are all too likely to encourage complacency with existing unjust structures of which our educational institutions are an example. Globally viewed, existing educational institutions function to increase the power of the rich at the expense of the poor. When they educate some of the poor, they separate those who are educated from the real needs of their fellows. For example, most education throughout the poorer nations directs its recipients to professional and bureaucratic jobs that are already oversupplied. It syphons off leadership from the peasant communities which are badly in need of help in organising themselves so as to take their destinies into their own hands and improve the base of their life-support systems. It makes the powerless even more dependent on inaccessible centres of power. Ivan Illich's shocking call for 'de-schooling society'[30] is in fact a reasoned and relevant proposal for dealing with a disastrous injustice. As the world currently understands 'education' it will not be by extending it but by curtailing it that progress toward justice will be possible.

If those of us engaged in teaching the privileged are to justify our work, it cannot be only by claiming that we enrich the experience of our students. That enrichment must be an appropriate enrichment, one that arouses an awareness of the real situation of the world and elicits solidarity with the oppressed. This need not preclude the assimilation of the great riches of the Western cultural tradition, but it should introduce the student to the spirit of critical transcendence of that tradition which is its most valuable heritage and which today points to a global horizon that the tradition has neglected or obscured.

By thinking through the meaning of our legacy, process theologians are led, no less than others, to the view that the special concern of the Christian, as of God, is with the liberation of the oppressed. The natural emphasis of process thought, however, is on finding ways for all to grow together in freedom and richness of experience. Even the service of others is best conceived as a way in which through responsible expression of concern for others, the freedom and quality of experience of the server is enhanced. The tension between this quest for mutuality and the centrality of the cross should not be concealed. It is a tension internal to the life of one who lives in the spirit of process theology.[31]

There is a fourth difference of equal practical importance. It can be illustrated by the problem of Israel which was posed before as a challenge to Metz. His form of political theology seems to call for an immediate solidarity with the oppressed, wherever they are, and regardless of the circumstances of the oppression. Whitehead's does not. In his view we should seek to remove obstacles to freedom whenever their removal does not reduce freedom elsewhere. This involves a rational, calculative approach which seems alien to Metz and which is certainly subject to distorted use. Every revolution can be opposed on the grounds that it will adversely affect someone's freedom, and arguments about how many will be affected how much and in what ways can function as a serious impediment to the struggle for justice.

Nevertheless, process theologians have no way to escape this need for calculative reflection and all the ambiguities it introduces. However oppressive the Arab people find the Jewish hegemony in Israel, we cannot immediately support their struggle for liberation without considering the consequences that would follow from its success. The contributions which the Jewish people make, often through their original and profound ideas, to the global extension and deepening of freedom and the horrendous injustices they have suffered over centuries at our Christian hands weigh heavily in our considerations. There are times when, with fear and dread, we will tolerate some measure of oppression for the sake of goals that are ultimately contributory to freedom, although we will not forget the self-deception with which we allow inescapable limitations on freedom to pass over into unnecessary cruelty.

In his account of the movement toward the abolition of slavery, Whitehead faced this problem squarely. In his view the long delay in the abolition of slavery after the introduction of the idea of the human soul does not reflect only human wilfulness and stubbornness in the pursuit of unjustified self-interest. It also reflects the fact that the extension of freedom and equality are not the only or even the most fundamental values. Even more fundamental is the survival of human community. More concretely, Whitehead speculates that the price for the abolition of slavery in the Roman Empire might well have been too high. He asks:

> Would Rome have been destroyed by a crusade for the abolition of slavery in the time of Cicero or in the time of Augustus? Throughout

the whole period of classical civilization the foundations of social order could scarcely sustain the weight upon them — the wars between states, the surrounding barbarians, the political convulsions, the evils of the slave system. In the age from the birth of Cicero to the accession of Augustus to undisputed power, the whole structure almost collapsed, before it had finished its appointed task. Even earlier, it had nearly met its fate, and later by a few centuries came the final collapse. It is impossible to doubt the effect of any vigorous effort for the immediate abolition of the only social system men knew. It may be better that the heavens should fall, but it is only folly to ignore the fact that they will fall.[32]

Political theologians seem, on the whole, to be willing for the heavens to fall.[33] Whitehead judged otherwise, and in this judgement most process theologians are likely, reluctantly, to follow. We need to appreciate the positive contributions of existing social structures as well as to be sensitive to their failures to embody the principles of freedom and equality. We need to recognise that no society will embody these perfectly. Hence, along with prophetic denunciation of the injustices which every society involves, we need to share in the consideration of the real alternatives confronting the society and in support for the best of the imperfect options available.

There is no doubt that this point can encourage support for existing structures which in fact should be overthrown. What now functions can always claim to have proven itself, whereas the proposals of revolutionaries have not. We must recognise the danger that 'realism' can be used to justify what in fact it does not justify. But we must recognise the danger that the abandonment of realism can lead to unjustifiable projects also. In the spirit of Niebuhr, we must hope that prophetic passion is not destroyed by realistic appraisals of the possible. It is the task of the Christian imagination to generate visions of what is actually possible that can give realism to efforts guided by the passion for justice. That imagination must be disciplined by a knowledge of political, social and economic theory. But it must not be restricted to the patterns into which the thought of the past has been channelled.[34]

IV

Chapters Three, Four and Five offered supplementation of what has been done by the German political theologians from the perspective of process theology. Chapters Six and Seven have criticised features of Metz's position and proposed an alternative. The net effect may appear to be the claim of superiority, for process thought over German political theology. That would be unfortunate.

As a process theologian I do believe that this tradition can contribute insights to the development and enlargement of political theology. I have argued this in some detail. But the deeper thesis of the book is the need for process theology for its own sake and for the sake of the gospel to become a political theology, a need unlikely to have been realised without the stimulus and challenge of the theologies of liberation and of political theology.

Looking back, many of us who stand in the tradition of process thought must recognise that quite unconsciously our work has largely expressed our position as white, middle-class, North American males. No doubt it still does. Even when the distortion introduced into our perceptions by this sociological situation was pointed out to us, we were slow to acknowledge it. Even now we tend to universalise judgements that are in fact shaped by quite particular and limited cultural experience. To force us to further self-criticism we need more external criticism, especially from Black, political and Latin American theologians.

The preceding chapters have indicated many disagreements in detail as to how a political theology is best formulated. They have accepted wholeheartedly the conviction that the call of the Christian is to participate in God's work toward the indivisible salvation of the whole world. No less inclusive a goal can be truly Christian in our day. The political theologians are also entirely correct in holding that commitment to this goal entails involvement in all dimensions of social and public life. It cannot be appropriately sought through an individualistic approach. Individuals must be called to share in the task. They must be assured of God's forgiving love in Jesus Christ. But such assurance that we are justified is not the full salvation for which we hope. We remain sinners bound up with a suffering and oppressed creation. It is for the whole world that God experienced death in Jesus and continues to suffer with us.

To understand Christian faith in this way is a great gain, but it is barely a beginning. Those Christians who agree that it is the indivisible salvation of the whole world to which we are committed may still disagree fundamentally as to what is required for its salvation.

Some believe that the defence of Christendom against atheistic Marxism is the most basic requirement. Others hold that the overthrow of capitalism is the absolute need, even if this entails the universal hegemony of the Soviet Union. Still others see hope only in the destruction of all forms of industrial civilisation and the return to much simpler forms of social organisation. The vast majority, of course, adopt none of these extreme views, but this does not mean that there is a consensus around some middle position.

Direct debate between advocates of alternative scenarios is rarely fruitful. But Christians can generally agree on one further step. If we are concerned with the salvation of the whole world, we have learned that we should listen to the various subjects of this salvation. We are learning that what has been seen from the perspective of white North Atlantic males is only a small part of what needs to be seen. Proposed solutions to global problems which are based only on the experience of the recently dominant group are unlikely to lead to the indivisible salvation of the whole world.

When the door is opened to a plurality of perspectives, confusion must be expected. The experience of Blacks in the United States has been quite different from that of peasants in Latin America. Both differ from that of North Atlantic women. As these voices were heard in the late sixties and throughout the seventies, the claims they made upon white, North Atlantic males seemed to be in marked conflict. Adjustments to one set of demands might be opposed by another group. But with surprising rapidity the three groups have moved toward a common front, one which brings a richer contribution to the whole than any could individually have made. Much of the credit here goes to the Theology of the Americas movement.[35]

But the work has just begun. We must see the world's reality and needs in a way that is informed by the experiences of all its people. Blacks, women and Latin Americans have much to contribute to this — but there are others. For example, we must not forget the experience of Jews who have suffered more than any others at the hand of Christians through nineteen centuries. A global vision that unites many groups of Christians at the expense of continued anti-Judaism will not do. Again, the flight of homosexuals from Cuba reminds us that a society committed to many forms of liberation may yet oppress some of its minorities. There are also the young and the old, the disabled and the emotionally disturbed, the genuises and the free spirits.

There are other vast groups to which we need to be attentive. Most of the people of the world are formed in their perceptions and hopes by religious traditions other than Judaism and Christianity. What they see is quite different from what we see. In the twentieth century, dialogue with representatives of other traditions has advanced greatly. But we have hardly begun to integrate what we are learning there with what the liberation theologians are teaching us.

Still more difficult but not less important is to consider the perspectives of the voiceless. Unless catastrophe intervenes, there will be future generations of human beings to whom our present policies are bequeathing an impoverished planet. There are other creatures with whom we are now sharing the planet to whose welfare many humanitarians appear quite indifferent. A global transformation that is insensitive to these voiceless ones would not be the salvation of the whole world!

The World Council of Churches has provided a forum for many voices including those who would speak for the voiceless. Slowly and painfully it moves toward a vision of a just, participatory, and sustainable society. Gradually it brings its own participants to the realisation of how deeply we will need to rethink our theology if we are to contribute to a saved world.[36] The work has just begun.

Individual thinkers, of course, are in the vanguard. Among those who are sensitive to the widest range of experiences and interests women are conspicuous. Rosemary Ruether has incorporated the concerns of women, Blacks and Latin Americans. She has also dealt passionately with Christian anti-Judaism.[37] And she, like many women, is deeply aware of the close relationship between human oppression and environmental destruction.[38] Her capacity to move toward a creative synthesis informed by all of this is encouraging for the future course of political theology.

The close relation between oppression of human beings and exploitation of nature has been richly documented by Carolyn Merchant in *The Death of Nature: Women, Ecology, and the Scientific Revolution*.[39] In particular she shows the anti-feminism that was involved in the shift of the image of nature from organism to machine with the accompanying concern to dominate nature. Merchant shows that a fundamental philosophical idea lies at the root of modern science and technological society. The many particular problems we face cannot be dealt with satisfactorily unless this, too, is challenged. She speaks here of 'the mechanistic view of nature, developed by the seventeenth-century natural philosophers and based on a Western mathematical tradition going back to Plato'.[40] 'This view assumes that nature can be divided into parts and that the parts can be rearranged to create other species of being.'[41]

Against this view she opposes holism, of which the most important expression today is the science of ecology. In this perspective 'the parts ... take their meaning from the whole. Each particular part is defined by and dependent on the total context'.[42] In this ecological view of a nature which includes human beings, nothing is wholly self-subsistent. Nothing satisfies the definition of a substance as 'a thing existing in such a manner that it has need of no other thing in order to exist'.[43] Each thing is what it is by virtue of its relationship to other things. With such an understanding we can see and experience nature as alive and all living things as having their own purposes and claims and values independently of human interests. We will again exist in a world of subjects rather than a world of objects, and such a world will call for a new type of science and a changed role for technology.[44] Compared with such a revolution the issues separating liberals and Marxists are relatively minor.

Much in the experience of Blacks, of Latin Americans, of Africans, of Hindus, and of Buddhists, as well as of women, favours this ecological view of nature against the mechanistic one. There is, therefore, some prospect that others seeking their own liberation may join the more far-sighted women in the recognition of the need to challenge the fundamental ideas on which our scientific-technological society has been built. The chief obstacle here is the real urgency of political action combined with impatience with speculative philosophy. But political theology cannot realise its goals without reopening these basic questions of the intellectual life. The effort to solve problems within a system so designed as inevitably to create such problems is doomed to frustration. The system itself must be uprooted beginning with its deep hold upon the common sense and imagination of each of us.

Although many 'conservative' Christians seem to be committed to the mechanistic view of nature with the accompanying 'supernaturalism' which separates God from the world, what they are conserving has little to do with the Bible. The Biblical vision has much to offer as an alternative to both mechanism and the organicism which it displaced. It offers us a picture of a world of interconnected and interdependent creatures in which human beings have particular but not exclusive privileges and responsibilities. The unity of this world is not that of an organism but of a creation. That is, the world has its unity in its relation to God. Finally, this relation is understood in terms of God's incarnation. In Christ God is the light and life of the world. There is no world apart from the divine enlightening and enlivening presence within it. But there is also no God, remote and self-existent, apart from concern for and action within the world. The Biblical vision of the world and of the relation of God and the world is not mechanical but ecological.

This Biblical vision comes to its ecstatic climax in Paul's apostrophe to universal salvation. Not all of us today will be able to take it as prosaic fact. But it has not lost its power to inspire as well as to mystify.

> For I reckon that the sufferings we now endure bear no comparison with the splendour, as yet unrevealed, which is in store for us. For the created universe waits with eager expectation for God's sons to be revealed. It was made the victim of frustration, not by its own choice, but because of him who made it so, yet always there was hope, because the universe itself is to be freed from the shackles of mortality and enter upon the liberty and splendour of the children of God. Up to the present, we know, the whole created universe groans in all its parts as if in the pangs of childbirth. Not only so, but even we, to whom the Spirit is given as firstfruits of the harvest to come, are groaning inwardly while we wait for God to make us his sons and set our whole body free. For we have been saved, though only in hope. Now to see is no longer to hope: why should a man endure and wait for what he already sees? But if we hope for something we do not yet see, then, in waiting for it, we show our endurance.[45]

NOTES

1 Johann Baptist Metz, *Faith in History and Society: Toward a Practical Fundamental Theology*, trans. David Smith (New York: Seabury Press, 1980), p. 6.
2 *Ibid.*
3 Karl Rahner and Johann B. Metz, *The Courage to Pray*, trans. Sarah O'Brien Twohig (New York: Crossroads, 1981), p. 27.
4 Metz, *Faith in History and Society*, p. 5.
5 *Ibid.*, p. 6.
6 *Ibid.*, p. 7.

7   *Ibid.*
8   *Ibid.*, p. 4.
9   *Ibid.*, p. 68.
10 *Ibid.*, p. 161.
11 *Ibid.*, p. 6.
12 *Ibid.*, p. 55.
13 *Ibid.*, p. 7.
14 For full-length treatment of the understanding of Christianity presented in this paragraph see my *Christ in a Pluralistic Age* (Philadelphia, Pa.: Westminster Press, 1975).
15 Johann Baptist Metz, 'The Church's social function in the light of a "Political theology"', trans. Theodore L. Westow, in *Faith and the World of Politics*, Concilium, vol. 36 (New York: Paulist Press, 1968), p. 14.
16 *Ibid.*, p. 18.
17 That Metz is fully sensitive to this is clear in his 'Ökumene nach Auschwitz; Zum Verhältnis von Christen und Juden in Deutschland', *Gott nach Auschwitz*, ed. Eugen Kogon and Johann Baptist Metz (Freiburg: Herder, 1978), pp. 121—44. This has been translated into English by Peter Mann as 'Christians and Jews after Auschwitz'. See Johann Baptist Metz, *The Emergent Church* (New York, Crossroad, 1981), pp. 17—35.
18 Reinhold Niebuhr, *The Irony of American History* (New York: Charles Scribner's Sons, 1952).
19 Teilhard de Chardin, *The Phenomenon of Man* (New York: Harper & Bros., 1959).
20 Arend Van Leeuwen, *Christianity in World History* (London: Edinburgh House Press, 1964).
21 Wolfhart Pannenberg, *Human Nature, Election, and History* (Philadelphia, Pa.: Westminster Press, 1977).
22 I contributed a book depicting history in terms of the emergence of structures of existence. John B. Cobb, Jr., *The Structure of Christian Existence* (Philadelphia, Pa.: Westminster Press, 1967).
23 Alfred North Whitehead, *Adventures of Ideas* (New York: The Free Press, 1933), p. 84.
24 *Ibid.*, p. 26.
25 *Ibid.*, p. 15.
26 Alfred North Whitehead, 'Liberty and the enfranchisement of women', *Process Studies* vol. 7, No. 1 (spring 1977), p. 37.
27 See chapter six in John B. Cobb, Jr. and David Ray Griffin, *Process Theology: an Introductory Exposition* (Philadelphia, Pa.: Westminster Press, 1976).
28 Metz, *Faith in History and Society*, p. 116.
29 See Whitehead, *Adventures of Ideas*, p. 95.
30 Ivan D. Illich, *Deschooling Society* (New York: Harper & Row, 1971).
31 Daniel Day Williams, *The Spirit and the Forms of Love* (New York: Harper & Row, 1968).

32 Whitehead, *Adventures of Ideas*, pp. 25—6.

33 Note, however, the sober realism of Jürgen Moltmann in 'An open letter to Jose Miguez Bonino', *Christianity and Crisis* (29 March 1976), p. 60. 'The necessity of a speedy and radical transformation of the socio-economic conditions can be understood by everyone as indisputable. But what use is the best revolutionary theory when the historical subject of the revolution is not at hand or is not yet ready?'

34 See Dorothee Sölle's call for fantasy in *Beyond Mere Obedience*, trans. Lawrence W. Denef (Minneapolis, Minn.: Augsburg, 1970); and Rubem Alves, *Tomorrow's Child: Imagination, Creativity, and the Rebirth of Culture* (New York: Harper & Row, 1972).

35 James Cone, the leading Black theologian, has gained a deep appreciation of the oppression of women and has found real solidarity with Third World theologians. 'The Gospel and the liberation of the poor', *The Christian Century* (18 Feb. 1981), pp. 162—6. Recently he has tentatively agreed to take part in a new proposed Christian-Buddhist dialogue.

36 See the report on 'Humanity, nature, and God' of the 1979 World Council of Churches Conference at MIT on Faith, Science and the Future. Paul Albrecht, ed., *Faith and Science in an Unjust World* (Geneva: World Council of Churches, 1980), vol. 2, pp. 28—36. Note the inclusion of comments on what can be learned from other religious traditions.

37 Rosemary Radford Ruether, *Faith and Fratricide: the Theological Roots of Anti-Semitism* (New York: Seabury Press, 1974).

38 Rosemary Radford Ruether, *New Women/New Earth: Sexist Ideologies and Human Liberation* (New York: Seabury Press, 1975).

39 Carolyn Merchant, *The Death of Nature: Women, Ecology, and the Scientific Revolution* (San Francisco, Calif.: Harper & Row, 1980).

40 *Ibid.*, p. 290.

41 *Ibid.*

42 *Ibid.*, p. 293.

43 René Descartes, *Principles of Philosophy*, Part 1: 51. The translation is from *Descartes: Philosophical Writings*, ed. and trans. Elizabeth Anscombe and Peter Thomas Geach (London: Thomas Nelson & Sons, 1954), p. 192. In this passage Descartes recognises that only God fully meets the requirements. He defines other substances as requiring nothing but God for their existence. For process theology God is not a substance either.

44 Birch and I have tried to contribute to this project in L. Charles Birch and John B. Cobb, Jr., *The Liberation of Life: From the Cell to the Community* (Cambridge: University Press, 1981).

45 Romans 8:18—25. New English Bible.